Working Words in Spelling

W9-BGG-637

Word-finder

A Quick Spelling Reference for Student Writers

Moore

Woodruff

Forest

Talbot

Talbot

Johnson

DiGiammarino

D.C. Heath and Company
HEATH Lexington, Massachusetts / Toronto, Ontario

Heath Wordfinder

George Moore
G. Willard Woodruff
Robert Forest

Richard Talbot
Ann Talbot
Donald Johnson

Frank DiGiammarino

Choosing the Best Word Form

The Heath Wordfinder contains over four thousand base words and over thirteen thousand other word forms. It is organized to help you quickly and easily find the form of the word that is the best one to use in your everyday writing. The Wordfinder is organized so that the entry form is usually the base form. Following this are other forms of each entry word with various endings, such as **–s**, **–ed**, **–ing**, **–er**, **–est**, **–ly**, **–es**, **–ment**, and **–tion**.

These endings or suffixes are important to us as writers. They help us to use the correct tense or part of speech. They are, however, more difficult to spell than the base words from which they originated. To help you with this difficulty, the Wordfinder shows most of the endings so you can be sure of their correct spellings when you use them in your everyday writing.

Using your Heath Wordfinder daily will help you become a more accurate and powerful speller.

Editor   Wanda Lankenner MacDonald
Designer   Eleanor Thayer
Production Coordinator   Joseph A. Hinckley

Copyright © 1990 by D.C. Heath and Company

Published simultaneously in Canada

Printed in the United States of America

International Standard Book Number: 0-669-20711-X

3   4   5   6   7   8   9   0

A

abandon abandons, abandoned, abandoning, abandonment

able abler, ablest, ability, abilities

about

above

absent absence, absences, absentee, absenteeism, absently

absolute absolutely, absoluteness

abstract abstracts, abstractly, abstractness

abundant abundantly, abundance, abundancy

accent accents, accented, accenting

accept accepts, accepted, accepting, acceptable, acceptably, acceptance, acceptability

accident accidents, accidental, accidentally

accommodate accommodates, accommodated, accommodating, accommodatingly, accommodative, accommodation, accommodator, accommodators

accompany accompanies, accompanied, accompanying, accompaniment, accompanist, accompanists

accomplish accomplishes, accomplished, accomplishing, accomplishable, accomplishment, accomplishments

accord accords, accorded, according, accordingly, accordance

account accounts, accounted, accounting, accountable, accountant, accountants

accurate accurately, accuracy, accurateness

accuse accuses, accused, accusing, accusingly, accuser, accusation, accusations

accustom accustoms, accustomed

ache aches, ached, aching

achieve achieves, achieved, achieving, achievable, achievement, achievements, achiever, achievers

acid acids, acidic, acidly, acidity, acidness

acknowledge acknowledges, acknowledged, acknowledging, acknowledgeable, acknowledgment, acknowledgments

acquaint acquaints, acquainted, acquainting, acquaintance, acquaintances

acquire acquires, acquired, acquiring

acre acres, acreage

across

act acts, acted, acting, action, actions, actor, actors, actress, actresses

active actively, activate, activates, activated, activating, activeness, activism, activist, activity, activities

actual actually, actualize, actualized, actualizes, actualizing, actuality, actualization, actualizations

acute acutely, acuteness

adapt adapts, adapted, adapting, adaptive, adaptable, adapter, adapters, adaptation, adaptations

add adds, added, adding, addend, addendum, adder, addition, additions, additional, additionally, additive, additives

address addresses, addressed, addressing

adequate adequately, adequacy, adequateness

adjourn adjourns, adjourned, adjourning, adjournment, adjournments

adjust adjusts, adjusted, adjusting, adjustable, adjustment, adjuster, adjusters

administer administers, administered, administering, administrate, administrative, administration, administrations, administrator, administrators

admire admires, admired, admiring, admirable, admirably, admiringly, admirability, admiration, admirer, admirers

admit admits, admitted, admitting, admittedly, admittance, admission, admissions

adopt adopts, adopted, adopting, adoptable, adopter, adoption, adoptions

advance advances, advanced, advancing, advancer, advancement, advancements

advantage advantages, advantageous, advantageously

adventure adventures, adventured,
adventuring, adventurer, adventurers,
adventurous, adventurously,
adventuresome

advertise advertises, advertised,
advertising, advertisement,
advertisements, advertiser, advertisers

advise advises, advised, advising, advice,
adviser, advisers

affair affairs

affect affects, affected, affecting,
affectionate, affectionately, affectation,
affection, affections

afford affords, afforded, affording,
affordable, affordably

afraid

after

afternoon afternoons

afterward afterwards

again

against

age ages, aged, aging

agent agents, agency, agencies

ago

agree agrees, agreed, agreeing, agreeable,
agreeably, agreeableness, agreement,
agreements, agreeability

agriculture agricultural, agriculturally

ahead

aid aids, aided, aiding

aim aims, aimed, aiming, aimless,
    aimlessly, aimlessness

air airs, aired, airing, airy

airport airports

aisle aisles

alarm alarms, alarmed, alarming,
    alarmingly

alike alikeness

alive

all

alley alleys

allow allows, allowed, allowing, allowable,
    allowably, allowance, allowances

all right

almost

alone

along

already

also

alter alters, altered, altering, alteration,
    alterations

although

altogether

always

ambassador ambassadors, ambassadorial,
    ambassadorship, ambassadorships

ambition ambitions, ambitionless, ambitious, ambitiously

ambulate ambulates, ambulated, ambulating, ambulation, ambulatory

ambulance ambulances

amend amends, amended, amending, amendable, amendment, amendments

America Americas, American, Americans, Americanism

ammunition ammunitions

among amongst

amount amounts, amounted, amounting

ample amply, ampleness

amuse amuses, amused, amusing, amusingly, amusable, amusement, amusements

an

analyze analyzes, analyzed, analyzing, analytic, analytical, analytically, analysis, analyses, analyst

ancestor ancestors, ancestral, ancestry, ancestries

anchor anchors, anchored, anchoring, anchorage, anchorages

ancient ancients, ancientness

and

anger angers, angered, angering, angry, angrier, angriest, angrily

angle angles, angled, angling

animal   animals

animate   animates, animated, animating, animation, animator, animators

ankle   ankles

anniversary   anniversaries

announce   announces, announced, announcing, announcement, announcements, announcer, announcers

annual   annuals, annually

another

answer   answers, answered, answering

ant   ants

anticipate   anticipates, anticipated, anticipating, anticipatory, anticipation

anxiety   anxieties, anxious, anxiously, anxiousness

any   anybody, anyhow, anyone, anything, anyway, anywhere

apartment   apartments

apiece

apology   apologies, apologize, apologizes, apologized, apologizing

apparent   apparently, apparentness

appeal   appeals, appealed, appealing, appealingly

appear   appears, appeared, appearing, appearance, appearances

appetite   appetites, appetize, appetizer, appetizers

apple apples

appliance appliances

apply applies, applied, applying, applicable, applicant, applicants, application, applications, applicator, applicators

appoint appoints, appointed, appointing, appointment, appointments

appreciate appreciates, appreciated, appreciating, appreciable, appreciative, appreciably, appreciation, appreciations

approach approaches, approached, approaching, approachable

approve approves, approved, approving, approvingly, approval, approvals

approximate approximates, approximated, approximating, approximately, approximation, approximations

April Apr.

apron aprons, aproned

are aren't

area areas

argue argues, argued, arguing, argument, arguments, argumentative

arithmetic arithmetical

arm arms

army armies

armor armors, armored, armory

around

arrange   arranges, arranged, arranging, arranger, arrangement, arrangements

arrest   arrests, arrested, arresting, arrester, arresters

arrive   arrives, arrived, arriving, arrival, arrivals

arrow   arrows

art   arts, artist, artists, artistic, artistically, artistry

article   articles

artificial   artificially, artificialness

as

ash   ashes, ashy

aside   asides

ask   asks, asked, asking

asleep

assemble   assembles, assembled, assembling, assemblage, assembly, assemblies, assembler, assemblers

assign   assigns, assigned, assigning, assignable, assigner, assignment, assignments

assist   assists, assisted, assisting, assistance, assistant, assistants

associate   associates, associated, associating, association, associations

assort   assorts, assorted, assorting, assortment, assortments

assume assumes, assumed, assuming, assumable, assumer, assumption, assumptions

assure assures, assured, assuring, assuredly, assurance, assurances, assurer, assurers

astonish astonishes, astonished, astonishing, astonishingly, astonishment

astronaut astronauts, astronautic, astronautics, astronautical

at

athlete athletes, athletic, athletically, athletics

atmosphere atmospheres, atmospheric, atmospherical, atmospherically

attach attaches, attached, attaching, attachable, attachment, attachments

attack attacks, attacked, attacking, attacker, attackers

attain attains, attained, attaining, attainable, attainment

attempt attempts, attempted, attempting

attend attends, attended, attending, attendance, attentive, attentively, attentiveness, attendant, attendants

attention attentions

attic attics

attitude attitudes

attorney attorneys

attract attracts, attracted, attracting, attractive, attractively, attractiveness, attraction, attractions

auction auctions, auctioned, auctioning, auctioneer, auctioneers

audience audiences

auditorium auditoriums

August Aug.

aunt aunts

author authors, authored, authoring

authority authorities, authorize, authorization, authoritarian, authoritative

automobile automobiles, auto

automate automates, automated, automating

automatic automation

autumn autumns

avail avails, availed, availing, available, availably, availableness, availability

avenue avenues, Ave.

average averages, averaged, averaging

aviation aviator, aviators

avoid avoids, avoided, avoiding, avoidable, avoidably, avoidance

await awaits, awaited, awaiting

awake awakes, awaked, awoke, awaking, awaken, awakens

aware awareness

away

away
awful awfully, awfulness
awkward awkwardly, awkwardness
ax axes, axed, axing

B

baby babies, babied, babying, babyish

back backs, backward, backwards

backfire backfires, backfired, backfiring, backfirings

bacteria bacterium

bad badly, badness

badge badges

bait baits, baited, baiting

bake bakes, baked, baking, baker, bakers, bakery, bakeries

balance balances, balanced, balancing, balancer

ball balls

ballet ballets, ballerina, ballerinas

balloon balloons, ballooned, ballooning

ballot ballots, balloted, balloting

banana bananas

band bands

bang bangs, banged, banging

banister banisters

bank banks, banked, banking, banker, bankers

bankrupt bankruptcy, bankruptcies, bankrupts, bankrupting

banner banners

banquet banquets, banqueted, banqueting

barbecue　barbecues, barbecued, barbecuing

bare　bares, bared, baring, barer, barest, barely, bareness

bargain　bargains, bargained, bargaining, bargainer, bargainers

baritone　baritones

bark　barks, barked, barking

barn　barns

barrel　barrels, barreled, barreling, barrelful, barrelfuls

base　bases, based, basing, basis, basic, basically

baseball　baseballs

basement　basements

basket　baskets

basketball　basketballs

bat　bats

bath　baths, bathing, bathed, bathe, bathes, bather, bathers

battery　batteries

battle　battles, battled, battling, battler, battlers

bazaar　bazaars

be　am, is, was, were, been, being

beach　beaches

bead　beads, beaded, beading

beam　beams, beamed, beaming

bean beans

bear bears, bore, borne, bearing, bearable, bearably, bearer, bearers

beast beasts, beastly

beat beats, beating, beaten, beater, beaters

beautiful beautifully, beauty, beautify, beautified, beautifying, beautification

because

become becomes, becoming, became

bed beds

bedroom bedrooms

bedtime bedtimes

bee bees

beef beefy

before

beg begs, begged, begging, beggar, beggars

begin begins, began, begun, beginning, beginner, beginners

behave behaves, behaved, behaving, behavior, behaviors, behavioral, behaviorally

behind

believe believes, believed, believing, believable, believably, believability, belief, beliefs

bell bells

belong belongs, belonged, belonging, belongings

15

below

belt belts, belted

bench benches

bend bends, bent, bending, bendable

beneath

benefit benefits, benefited, benefiting, beneficial, beneficiary, beneficiaries

berry berries

beside

best better

bestow bestows, bestowed, bestowing, bestowal

bet bets, betted, betting, bettor, bettors

betray betrays, betrayed, betraying, betrayer, betrayal

between

bewilder bewilders, bewildered, bewildering, bewilderingly, bewilderment, bewilderments

beyond

bicycle bicycles, bicycled, bicycling, bicycler, bicyclist, bicyclists

bid bids, bidder, bidding

big bigger, biggest

bike bikes, biked, biking

bill bills, billed, billing

bind binds, binder, binding

bird birds

birth   births

birthday   birthdays

biscuit   biscuits

bite   bites, biting, bit, bitten, biter, biters

bitter   bitterly, bitterness

black   blacker, blackest

blade   blades

blame   blames, blamed, blaming, blameless

blanket   blankets, blanketed, blanketing

blast   blasts, blasted, blasting

blaze   blazes, blazed, blazing

blimp   blimps

blind   blinds, blinded, blinding, blindly, blindness

blizzard   blizzards

block   blocks, blocked, blocking, blocker, blockers

blood   bleed, bleeds, bleeding, bled, bloody, bloodier, bloodiest, bloodiness

bloom   blooms, bloomed, blooming, bloomer, bloomers

blossom   blossoms, blossomed, blossoming, blossomless

blouse   blouses

blow   blows, blew, blown, blowing, blower, blowers

blue   bluer, bluest

bluff   bluffs, bluffed, bluffing, bluffer, bluffers

board   boards, boarded, boarding, boarder

boat   boats, boating

body   bodies, bodily

boil   boils, boiled, boiling, boiler, boilers

bond   bonds, bonded, bonding, bondage

book   books

bookkeeping   bookkeeper, bookkeepers

boot   boots

border   borders, bordered, bordering

bore   bores, bored, boring, boredom

born

borrow   borrows, borrowed, borrowing, borrower, borrowers

both

bother   bothers, bothered, bothering

bottom   bottoms, bottomless

bough   boughs

boulevard   boulevards

bound   bounds, bounded, bounding, boundless, boundary, boundaries

bouquet   bouquets

bow   bows, bowed, bowing

bowl   bowls, bowled, bowling, bowler, bowlers

box   boxed, boxing, boxer, boxers

boy boys

bracelet bracelets

braid braids, braided, braiding

brain brains, brainy, brainier, brainiest, brainless

brake brakes, braked, braking

branch branches, branched, branching

brass brasses, brassy

brave braver, bravest, braves, braved, braving, bravely, braveness, bravery

bread breads

break breaks, broke, broken, breaking, breakable, breaker, breakers

breakfast breakfasts, breakfasted, breakfasting

breath breaths, breather, breathless, breathlessly, breathlessness, breathe, breathes, breathed, breathing, breathable

briar briars

brick bricks, bricked, bricking

bridge bridges, bridged, bridging

brief briefer, briefest, briefs, briefed, briefing, briefly, briefness

bright brighter, brightest, brighten, brightly, brightness

brilliance brilliant, brilliantly

bring brings, brought, bringing

broad　broader, broadest, broaden, broadens, broadened, broadening, broadly, broadness

brook　brooks

brother　brothers

brown　browner, brownest

browse　browses, browsed, browsing, browser, browsers

bruise　bruises, bruised, bruising

brush　brushes, brushed, brushing

bucket　buckets

bud　buds, budded, budding

budget　budgets, budgeted, budgeting, budgetary

bug　bugs

build　builds, built, building, buildings, builder, builders

bull　bulls, bully, bullies, bullied, bullying

bulletin　bulletins

bullpen　bullpens

bump　bumps, bumped, bumping, bumper, bumpers, bumpy

bundle　bundles, bundled, bundling, bundler, bundlers

bunny　bunnies

burden　burdens, burdened, burdening, burdensome

burglar　burglars, burglary, burglarize, burglarizes, burglarized

bureau   bureaus

bureaucrat   bureaucratic,
   bureaucratically, bureaucracy

burlap

burn   burns, burned, burnt, burning,
   burner, burners

burst   bursts, burst, bursting

bury   buries, buried, burying, burial

bus buses

bush   bushes, bushy

bushel   bushels, busheled, busheling

bustle   bustles, bustled, bustling

busy   busies, busied, busying, busier,
   busiest, busyness, business, businesses

but

butter   butters, buttered, buttering

button   buttons, buttoned, buttoning

buy   buys, bought, buying, buyer, buyers

by

by-product   by-products

C

cabbage cabbages

cabin cabins

cabinet cabinets

cable cables, cabled

cafeteria cafeterias, cafe, cafes

cage cages

cake cakes

calamity calamities, calamitous, calamitously

calculate calculates, calculated, calculating, calculation, calculations, calculator, calculators

calendar calendars

caliber calibers, calibrate, calibrates, calibrated, calibrating, calibration, calibrator

calf calves

call calls, called, calling, caller, callers

calm calms, calmed, calming, calmer, calmest, calmly, calmness

camel camels

camp camps, camped, camping, camper, campers

campaign campaigns, campaigned, campaigning, campaigner, campaigners

campus campuses

can cannot, can't, could

canal canals

cancel cancels, cancelled, cancelling, cancellation, cancellations

candidate candidates, candidacy, candidacies

candle candles

candy candies

cane canes

canister canisters

canoe canoes, canoed, canoeing

canvas canvases

canvass canvasses, canvassed, canvassing, canvasser, canvassers

canyon canyons

cap caps

capable capably, capableness, capability, capabilities

capacity capacities

cape capes

capital capitals, capitalize, capitalizes, capitalized, capitalizing, capitalization, capitalist, capitalists

capitol capitols

captain captains, captained, captaining

capture captures, captured, capturing, captive, captives, captivity, captor, captors

car cars

carbon carbons

card cards

care cares, cared, caring, careful, carefully, carefulness

career careers

careless carelessly, carelessness

carload carloads

carnival carnivals

carpet carpets, carpeted, carpeting

carriage carriages

carry carries, carried, carrying, carrier, carriers

cart carts

case cases, cased, casing, casings

cash cashes, cashed, cashing, cashier, cashiers

cassette cassettes

castaway castaways

castle castles

cat cats, catty

catalog catalogs, cataloged, cataloging, cataloger, catalogers

catch catches, caught, catching, catcher, catchers

category categories, categorize, categorizes, categorized, categorizing, categoric, categorical, categorically, categorization, categorizations

cattle

cause causes, caused, causing, causable

caution cautions, cautioned, cautioning, cautionary, cautious, cautiously, cautiousness

cease ceases, ceased, ceasing, ceaseless, ceaselessly

cedar cedars

ceiling ceilings

celebrate celebrates, celebrated, celebrating, celebrant, celebration, celebrations

celebrity celebrities

cellar cellars

cement cements, cemented, cementing

cemetery cemeteries

census censuses

cent cents

center centers, centered, centering, central, centralize, centralizes, centralized, centralizing

centimeter centimeters

century centuries

cereal cereals

ceremony ceremonies, ceremonial

certain certainly, certainty

certify certifies, certified, certifying, certifiable, certifiably, certificate, certificates, certification, certifications

chain chains, chained, chaining

chair   chairs

chairperson   chairpersons

chalk   chalks, chalked, chalking, chalky

challenge   challenges, challenged, challenging, challengeable, challenger, challengers

chamber   chambers, chambered

champion   champions, championed, championing, championship, championships

chance   chances, chanced, chancing

change   changes, changed, changing, changeable, changeably, changeless, changer, changers

channel   channels, channeled, channeling

chapter   chapters

character   characters, characteristic, characteristics, characteristically, characterize, characterization, characterizations

charge   charges, charged, charging, chargeable, charger

charity   charities, charitable, charitably, charitableness

charm   charms, charmed, charming, charmer, charmingly

chart   charts, charted, charting

chase   chases, chased, chasing, chaser, chasers

chatter   chatters, chattered, chattering, chatterer, chatterers

cheap   cheaper, cheapest, cheapen, cheapens, cheapened, cheaply, cheapness

cheat   cheats, cheated, cheating, cheater, cheaters

check   checks, checked, checking, checker, checkers

cheer   cheers, cheered, cheering, cheery, cheerier, cheeriest, cheeriness

cheerful   cheerfully

cheese   cheeses, cheesy

chemistry   chemistries, chemical, chemicals, chemically, chemist, chemists

cherish   cherishes, cherished, cherishing

cherry   cherries

chest   chests

chew   chews, chewed, chewing, chewy, chewier, chewiest

chicken   chickens

chief   chiefs, chiefly, chieftain, chieftains

child   children, childish, childlike, childhood, childhoods

chill   chills, chilled, chilling, chilly

chimney   chimneys

chocolate   chocolates, chocolaty

choir   choirs

choice   choices, choicer, choicest

choose chooses, chose, choosing, chosen, choosy, chooser, choosier, choosiest, choosiness

chop chops, chopped, chopping, chopper

chorus choruses, chorused, chorusing, choral

circle circles, circled, circling, circular

circuit circuits, circuited, circuiting, circuitous, circuitously, circuitry, circuitries

circulate circulates, circulated, circulating, circulation, circulator, circulatory

circumference circumferential

circumstance circumstances, circumstanced, circumstantial, circumstantially

circus circuses

citizen citizens, citizenry, citizenship

city cities

civil civilly, civilian, civilians, civilize, civilizes, civilized, civilizing, civilization, civilizations

claim claims, claimed, claiming, claimable, claimant, claimants

clammy clammier, clammiest, clamminess

clamor clamors, clamored, clamoring, clamorous, clamorously

clap claps, clapped, clapping

class classes, classed, classical, classifier, classify, classifies, classified, classifying, classification, classifications

clay

clean cleans, cleaned, cleaning, cleaner, cleaners, cleanest

clear clearer, clearest, clearly, clears, cleared, clearing, clearness, clarity

clerk clerks, clerked, clerking, clerical

clever cleverer, cleverest, cleverly, cleverness

cliff cliffs

climate climates, climatic

climax climaxes, climaxed, climaxing, climactic

climb climbs, climbed, climbing, climber, climbers

clock clocks

close closes, closed, closing, closer, closest, closely, closeness

closet closets

cloth cloths, clothe, clothes, clothed, clothing

cloud clouds, clouded, clouding, cloudy, cloudiness

clown clowns, clowned, clowning, clownish

club clubs, clubbed, clubbing

cluster clusters, clustered, clustering

coach coaches, coached, coaching

coal coals

coarse coarser, coarsest, coarsen, coarsened, coarsely, coarseness

coast coasts, coasted, coasting, coastal, coaster, coasters

coat coats

cocoa

cocoon cocoons

coin coins, coined, coining, coinage, coinages

coincide coincides, coincided, coinciding, coincident, coincidental, coincidently, coincidentally, coincidence, coincidences

cold colder, coldest, colds

collar collars, collared, collaring

collect collects, collected, collecting, collectable, collector, collectors, collection, collections

college colleges, collegiate, collegian, collegians

colonel colonels

colony colonies, colonize, colonizes, colonized, colonizing, colonization, colonial, colonially, colonialism, colonist, colonists

color colors, colored, coloring, colorful, colorfully

colossal colossally, colossus

colt colts

column columns, columned, columnist, columnists

comb combs, combed, combing

combine combines, combined, combining, combination, combinations

combust combusts, combusted, combusting, combustible, combustion

come comes, came, coming

comet comets

comfort comforts, comforted, comforting, comfortable, comfortably, comfortableness, comforter, comforters

command commands, commanded, commanding, commander, commandment, commandments

commence commences, commenced, commencing, commencement, commencements

commend commends, commended, commending, commendable, commendably, commendation, commendations

comment comments, commented, commenting, commentator, commentators

commerce commercial, commercials, commercially, commercialism, commercialization, commercializations

commission commissions, commissioned, commissioning, commissioner, commissioners

commit commits, committed, committing, committedly, commitment, commitments, committal

31

committee   committees

common   commoner, commonest, commonly, commonness

communicate   communicates, communicated, communicating, communication, communications, communicator, communicators

community   communities

commute   commutes, commuted, commuting, commuter, commuters

companion   companions, companionable, companionship, companionships

company   companies

compare   compares, compared, comparing, comparable, comparably, comparative, comparatively, comparison, comparisons

compass   compasses

compel   compels, compelled, compelling, compellingly

compensate   compensates, compensated, compensating, compensation, compensative, compensatory, compensator, compensators

compete   competes, competed, competing, competitive, competitively, competition, competitions, competitor, competitors, competitiveness

competent   competently, competence, competency, competencies

complain   complains, complained, complaining, complainant, complainer, complainers

complement complements, complemented, complementing, complementary

complete completes, completed, completing, completely, completeness, completion, completions

complex complexes, complexly, complexity, complexities

compliment compliments, complimented, complimenting, complimentary

comply complies, complied, complying, compliant, compliantly, compliance

compose composes, composed, composing, composite, composer, composition, compositions

comprehend comprehends, comprehended, comprehending, comprehensible, comprehension, comprehensive, comprehensiveness

compromise compromises, compromised, compromising, compromisingly, compromiser, compromisers

compute computes, computed, computing, computerize, computer, computers

conceal conceals, concealed, concealing, concealable, concealment

conceit conceits, conceited, conceiting, conceitedly, conceitedness

concern concerns, concerned, concerning

concert concerts, concerto, concertos

conclude concludes, concluded, concluding, conclusive, conclusively, conclusion, conclusions, conclusiveness

concrete concretes, concretely, concreteness

condemn condemns, condemned, condemning, condemnable, condemnation

condition conditions, conditioned, conditioning, conditional, conditionally, conditioner, conditioners

conduct conducts, conducted, conducting, conductible, conductive, conductibility, conductivity, conduction, conductor, conductors

confer confers, conferred, conferring, conference, conferences

confide confides, confided, confiding, confident, confidently, confidential, confidentially, confidant, confidants, confidence, confidences, confidentiality

confine confines, confined, confining, confinement, confinements

confirm confirms, confirmed, confirming, confirmation, confirmations

conflict conflicts, conflicted, conflicting

confuse confuses, confused, confusing, confusingly, confusedly, confusion, confusions

congratulate congratulates, congratulated, congratulating, congratulatory, congratulation, congratulations

congress congresses, congressional

connect connects, connected, connecting, connective, connector, connectors, connection, connections

conquer conquers, conquered, conquering, conqueror, conquerors

conscience consciences, conscientious, conscientiously

conscious consciously, consciousness

consent consents, consented, consenting

consequent consequently, consequential, consequentially, consequence, consequences

consider considers, considered, considering, consideration, considerations, considerable, considerably, considerate, considerately

consist consists, consisted, consisting, consistent, consistently, consistence, consistency, consistencies

conspicuous conspicuously, conspicuousness

constant constants, constantly, constancy

constitute constitutes, constituted, constituting, constitution, constitutions, constitutional, constitutionally

construct constructs, constructed, constructing, construction, constructions, constructive, constructively

consult consults, consulted, consulting, consultation, consultations, consultant, consultants

consume consumes, consumed, consuming, consumable, consumption, consumer, consumers

contact contacts, contacted, contacting

contain contains, contained, containing, containable, containment, container, containers

contemplate contemplates, contemplated, contemplating

contemporary contemporaries

content contents, contented, contentedly, contentment, contentments

contest contests, contestant, contestants

continent continents, continental

continue continues, continued, continuing, continual, continually, continuous, continuously, continuance, continuation, continuations

contract contracts, contracted, contracting, contraction, contractions, contractor, contractors

contradict contradicts, contradicted, contradicting, contradictable, contradictory, contradiction, contradictions

contrary contrarily, contrariness

contrast contrasts, contrasted, contrasting, contrastable

contribute contributes, contributed, contributing, contributor, contributors, contribution, contributions

control controls, controlled, controlling, controllable, controller, controllers

controversy controversies, controversial, controversially

convene convenes, convened, convening

convenience conveniences, convenient, conveniently

convention conventions

converse converses, conversed, conversing, conversation, conversations, conversational, conversationalist, conversely

convey conveys, conveyed, conveying, conveyable, conveyance, conveyances, conveyor, conveyors

convince convinces, convinced, convincing, convincingly

cook cooks, cooked, cooking, cooker

cookie cookies

cool cools, cooled, cooling, cooler, coolest

cooperate cooperates, cooperated, cooperating, cooperative, cooperatively, cooperativeness, cooperation, cooperations

copper coppered, coppery

copy copies, copied, copying, copier, copiers

corn

corner corners, cornered, cornering

cornerstone cornerstones

corporation corporations, corporate, corporately

correct corrects, corrected, correcting, correction, corrections, correctly, correctness

correspond   corresponds, corresponded, corresponding, correspondence, correspondent, correspondents

cost   costs, costing, costly

costume   costumes, costumed, costuming

cough   coughs, coughed, coughing

could   couldn't

council   councils, councilor, councilors

counsel   counsels, counseled, counseling, counselor, counselors

count   counts, counted, counting, countless, countlessly, counter, counters

counteract   counteracts, counteracted, counteracting, counteractive, counteraction, counteractions

country   countries

county   counties

coupon   coupons

courage   courageous, courageously

course   courses, coursed

court   courts, courted, courting

courtesy   courtesies, courteous, courteously

cousin   cousins

cover   covers, covered, covering

cow   cows

coward   cowards, cowardly, cowardliness

crack   cracks, cracked, cracking, cracker, crackers

crash   crashes, crashed, crashing

crawl   crawls, crawled, crawling, crawler, crawlers

crazy   crazier, craziest, crazily, craziness

cream   creams, creamed, creamy

create   creates, created, creating, creation, creations, creative, creatively, creativeness, creativity, creator, creators

creature   creatures

credence   credential, credentials

credit   credits, credited, crediting, creditor, creditors

creek   creeks

creep   creeps, crept, creeping, creeper, creepier, creepiest, creepily, creepiness, creepy

crime   crimes, criminal, criminals, criminally

crimson   crimsons, crimsoned

crisis   crises

criticize   criticizes, criticized, criticizing, critical, critically, critic, critics, criticism, criticisms, criticizer, critique, critiques

crop   crops, cropped, cropping

cross   crosses, crossed, crossing

crouch   crouches, crouched, crouching

crowd crowds, crowded, crowding

cruel crueler, cruelest, cruelly, cruelty, cruelties, cruelness

crush crushes, crushed, crushing, crushable, crusher, crushers

cry cries, cried, crying, crier, criers

crystal crystals, crystallize

cultivate cultivates, cultivated, cultivating, cultivation, cultivator, cultivators

cunning cunningly, cunningness

cup cups

curious curiously, curiosity, curiosities, curiousness

current currents, currently

curtain curtains, curtained

curve curves, curved, curving

cushion cushions, cushioned, cushioning

custody custodies, custodial, custodian, custodians, custodianship, custodianships

custom customs, customary, customize, customizes, customized, customizing, customer, customers

cut cuts, cutting, cutter, cutters

cute cuter, cutest, cutely, cuteness

cyclone cyclones, cyclonic

cylinder cylinders, cylindric, cylindrical, cylindrically

D

dad dads, daddy

daily dailies

damage damages, damaged, damaging

dance dances, danced, dancing, dancer, dancers

danger dangers, dangerous, dangerously

dare dares, dared, daring, daringly

dark darker, darkest, darkish, darkly, darken, darkens, darkened, darkening, darkness

dash dashes, dashed, dashing

daughter daughters

dawn dawns, dawned, dawning

day days

deaf deafen, deafens, deafened, deafening, deafness

deal deals, dealt, dealing, dealings, dealer, dealers

dear dearer, dearest

death deaths, deathly

debate debates, debated, debating, debatable

debt debts, debtor, debtors

decade decades

deceive deceives, deceived, deceiving, deceit, deceitful, deceivable, deceptive, deceitfully, deceivingly, deceptively, deceitfulness, deception

December Dec.

decent decently, decency

decide decides, decided, deciding, decidedly, decisive, decisively, decision, decisions

decimal decimals

deck decks, decked, decking

declare declares, declared, declaring, declarative, declaration, declarations

decline declines, declined, declining, declinable

decorate decorates, decorated, decorating, decorator, decorators, decoration, decorations, decorative, decoratively, decorativeness

deed deeds, deeded

deep deeper, deepest, deeply, deepen

defeat defeats, defeated, defeating, defeatist

defect defects, defected, defecting, defective, defectively, defection, defections, defectiveness, defector, defectors

defend defends, defended, defending, defendable, defendant, defendants, defender, defenders

defense defenses, defensive, defensively, defensiveness, defenseless

define defines, defined, defining, definable, definite, definitely, definition, definitive, definitions

defy defies, defied, defying, defiant, defiantly, defiance

delay   delays, delayed, delaying

delicate   delicately, delicateness, delicacy, delicacies

delicious   deliciously, deliciousness

delight   delights, delighted, delightedly, delightful, delightfully, delightfulness

delirious   deliriously, delirium

deliver   delivers, delivered, delivering, deliverable, delivery, deliveries

demand   demands, demanded, demanding

democracy   democracies, democrat, democrats, democratic, democratically

demonstrate   demonstrates, demonstrated, demonstrating, demonstrator, demonstrators, demonstrative, demonstratively, demonstration, demonstrations

den   dens

dense   denser, densest, densely, denseness, density

dentist   dentists, dental, dentally, dentistry

deny   denies, denied, denying, denial, deniable

depart   departs, departed, departing, departure, departures

department   departments, departmental, departmentally

depend   depends, depended, depending, dependable, dependably, dependence, dependency, dependent, dependents

deposit deposits, deposited, depositing, depositor, depositors

depot depots

depth depths

descend descends, descended, descending, descendant, descendants, descender, decenders, descent

describe describes, described, describing, describable, descriptive, descriptively, description, descriptions

desert deserts, deserted, deserting, deserter, deserters, desertion, desertions

deserve deserves, deserved, deserving, deservedly

design designs, designed, designing, designer, designers

desire desires, desired, desiring, desirable, desirably, desirous, desirously

desk desks

desolate desolated, desolately, desolateness, desolation

despair despairs, despaired, despairing, despairingly

desperate desperately, desperateness, desperation

despise despises, despised, despising, despicable, despicably

dessert desserts

destine destines, destined, destining, destiny, destination, destinations

destroy destroys, destroyed, destroying, destroyer, destroyers

destruct destructs, destructed, destructing, destructive, destructible, destruction

determine determines, determined, determining, determinedly, determinable, determination, determinant, determinate

detour detours, detoured, detouring

develop develops, developed, developing, development, developments, developmental, developmentally, developer, developers

devour devours, devoured, devouring, devouringly

diameter diameters

diamond diamonds

dictionary dictionaries

die dies, died, dying

diet diets, dieted, dieting, dietary, dietetic, dieter, dieters, dietician, dieticians

differ differs, differed, differing, different, differently, difference, differences

difficult difficultly, difficulty, difficulties

dig digs, dug, digging, digger, diggers

digest digests, digested, digesting, digestible, digestion, digestive

dignity dignify, dignifies, dignified, dignifying, dignitary, dignitaries

dilapidate dilapidates, dilapidated, dilapidating, dilapidation

dilute   dilutes, diluted, diluting, dilution, dilutions

dim   dims, dimmed, dimming, dimly, dimmer, dimmest, dimness

dime   dimes

diminish   diminishes, diminished, diminishing, diminishable, diminutive

dine   dines, dined, dining, diner

dinner   dinners

dinosaur   dinosaurs

dip   dips, dipped, dipping, dipper, dippers

diploma   diplomas, diplomacy, diplomat, diplomats

direct   directs, directed, directing, directly, direction, directions, directional, directness, director, directors, directory, directorship

dirt   dirty, dirtier, dirtiest, dirties, dirtied, dirtying

disagree   disagreeable, disagreement, disagreements

disappear   disappears, disappeared, disappearing, disappearance

disappoint   disappoints, disappointed, disappointing, disappointment, disappointments

disaster   disasters, disastrous, disastrously

discipline   disciplines, disciplined, disciplining, disciplinary, disciplinarian, disciplinarians

disconnect disconnects, disconnected, disconnecting, disconnectedly, disconnection

discontinue discontinues, discontinued, discontinuing

discover discovers, discovered, discovering, discovery

discuss discusses, discussed, discussing, discussable, discussion, discussions

disease diseases, diseased

disgrace disgraces, disgraced, disgracing, disgraceful, disgracefully

disgust disgusts, disgusted, disgusting, disgustedly

dish dishes

dislike dislikes, disliked, disliking, dislikable

dislodge dislodges, dislodged, dislodging, dislodgment

dismal dismally

dismiss dismisses, dismissed, dismissing, dismissal

dispense dispenses, dispensed, dispensing, dispensable, dispensation, dispensary, dispenser, dispensers

dispose disposes, disposed, disposing, disposal, disposable, disposals, disposition, dispositions

displease displeases, displeased, displeasing, displeasingly, displeasure, displeasures

dispute   disputes, disputed, disputing, disputable, disputably

disrupt   disrupts, disrupted, disrupting, disruptive, disruptively, disruption, disruptions

dissatisfy   dissatisfies, dissatisfied, dissatisfying, dissatisfactory, dissatisfaction

distant   distantly, distance

distinct   distinctly, distinctive, distinctively, distinction, distinctions, distinctiveness, distinctness

distinguish   distinguishes, distinguished, distinguishing, distinguishable

distribute   distributes, distributed, distributing, distributable, distribution, distributional, distributive, distributively

district   districts

disturb   disturbs, disturbed, disturbing, disturbingly, disturbance, disturbances

ditch   ditches, ditched, ditching

dive   dives, dived, diving, diver

divide   divides, divided, dividing, divisible, divider, dividend, division, divisions, divisor

do   did, does, done, doing, didn't, doesn't, don't, doer

doctor   doctors, doctored, doctoring, Dr.

document   documents, documented, documenting, documentation, documentations, documentary

dog dogs

doll dolls

dollar dollars

domestic domestics, domestically

donate donates, donated, donating, donation, donations, donor, donors

door doors

dose doses, dosage, dosages

dot dots, dotted, dotting

double doubles, doubled, doubling, doubly

doubt doubts, doubted, doubting, doubtingly, doubtable, doubtful, doubtfully, doubtfulness, doubtless, doubtlessly, doubtlessness, doubter, doubters

dove doves

down

downstairs

dozen dozens

drab drabber, drabbest, drably, drabness

draft drafts, drafted, drafting

drag drags, dragged, dragging

drain drains, drained, draining

drama dramatic, dramatical, dramatically, dramatics, dramatist, dramatists, dramatize, dramatizes, dramatizing, dramatization

drape drapes, draped, draping, drapery, draperies

draw   draws, drew, drawn, drawing, drawings

drawer   drawers

dream   dreams, dreamed, dreamt, dreaming, dreamer, dreamers, dreamy

dress   dresses, dressed, dressing, dressy

dresser   dressers

drill   drills, drilled, drilling

drink   drinks, drank, drunk, drinking, drinker, drinkers

drive   drives, drove, driving, driven, driver, drivers

drop   drops, dropped, dropping, dropper, droppers

drought   droughts

drown   drowns, drowned, drowning

drum   drums, drummed, drumming, drummer, drummers

dry   dries, dried, drying, drier, driest, dryly, dryness

dual   dually, dualistic, dualistically, dualism, duality

duck   ducks, ducked, ducking, duckling

due   dues

duplicate   duplicates, duplicated, duplicating, duplication, duplicator, duplicators

during

dust dusts, dusted, dusting, dusty, duster, dusters

duty duties, dutiful, dutifully

E

each

eager eagerly, eagerness

ear ears

early earlier, earliest

earn earns, earned, earning, earnings, earner, earners

earnest earnestly, earnestness

earth earthy, earthen, earthly

ease eases, eased, easing

east eastern, easterner, eastward, easterly

easy easier, easiest, easily, easiness

easygoing easygoingness

eat eats, ate, eaten, eating

echo echoes, echoed, echoing

economy economies, economize, economizes, economized, economizing, economic, economics, economical, economically, economist, economists

edge edges, edged, edging, edgy

edit edits, edited, editing, editorial, editorials, editorially, edition, editions, editor, editors

educate educates, educated, educating, educator, educators, education, educations, educational

effect effects, effected, effecting, effective, effectively, effectiveness, effectual, effectually

efficient   efficiently, efficiency

effort   efforts, effortless, effortlessly

egg eggs

eight   eights, eighth

eighteen   eighteenth, eighteenths

eighty   eighties, eightieth

either

elaborate   elaborates, elaborated, elaborating, elaborative, elaborately, elaborateness, elaboration

elapse   elapses, elapsed, elapsing

elbow   elbows, elbowed, elbowing

elect   elects, elected, electing, elective, electively, elector, electors, electoral, electorate, election, elections, electioneer

electricity   electric, electrical, electrify, electrifies, electrified, electrifying, electrocute, electrocutes, electrocuted, electrician, electricians

elegance   elegances, elegant, elegantly

element   elements

elephant   elephants

elevate   elevates, elevated, elevating, elevation, elevations

elevator   elevators

eleven   elevens, eleventh

eligible   eligibly, eligibility

eliminate   eliminates, eliminated, eliminating, elimination, eliminations

else

embarrass embarrasses, embarrassed, embarrassing, embarrassingly, embarrassment

emerge emerges, emerged, emerging, emergent, emergence, emergency, emergencies

emotion emotions, emotional, emotionally, emotionalism

emphasize emphasizes, emphasized, emphasizing, emphatic, emphatically, emphasis

empire empires, emperor, emperors, empress, empresses

employ employs, employed, employing, employable, employee, employees, employer, employers, employment

empty empties, emptied, emptying, emptiness

enable enables, enabled, enabling, enabler, enablers

enclose encloses, enclosed, enclosing, enclosure, enclosures

encounter encounters, encountered, encountering

encourage encourages, encouraged, encouraging, encouragingly, encouragement

end ends, ended, ending, endless

endorse endorses, endorsed, endorsing, endorser, endorsers, endorsement, endorsements

endure endures, endured, enduring, enduringly, endurable, endurably, endurance

enemy enemies

energy energies, energize, energizes, energized, energizing, energizer, energetic, energetically

enforce enforces, enforced, enforcing, enforceable, enforcer, enforcers, enforcement

engage engages, engaged, engaging, engagingly, engagement, engagements

engine engines, engineer, engineers, engineered, engineering

England English

enjoy enjoys, enjoyed, enjoying, enjoyable, enjoyably, enjoyment

enlarge enlarges, enlarged, enlarging, enlarger, enlargement, enlargements

enormous enormously, enormousness, enormity

enough

enter enters, entered, entering, entrance, entrances, entrant, entrants

entertain entertains, entertained, entertaining, entertainingly, entertainment, entertainer, entertainers

enthusiasm enthusiastic, enthusiastically, enthusiast, enthusiasts

entire entirely, entireness, entirety

envelope envelopes

envy   envies, envied, envying, envious,
  enviously, enviable, enviably

equal   equals, equaled, equaling, equality,
  equalize, equalizer, equalizers, equally

equip   equips, equipped, equipping,
  equipment

erect   erects, erected, erecting, erectly

erode   erodes, eroded, eroding, erosion

error   errors, errorless

escapade   escapades

escape   escapes, escaped, escaping, escapee,
  escapees

especially

essay   essays, essayist, essayists

essence   essences, essential, essentials,
  essentially

establish   establishes, established,
  establishing, establishment,
  establishments

estate   estates

estimate   estimates, estimated, estimating,
  estimation, estimations, estimator,
  estimators

even   evened, evenly, evenness, evener

evening   evenings

event   events, eventful, eventfully,
  eventual, eventually, eventuality

ever

every everybody, everyone, everything, everywhere

evidence evidences, evidenced, evidencing, evidential

evident evidently

evil evils, eviler, evilest, evilly, evilness

exact exactly, exactness

examine examines, examined, examining, exam, examination, examinations, examiner

example examples

exceed exceeds, exceeded, exceeding, exceedingly

excel excels, excelled, excelling, excellence, excellency, excellent, excellently

except excepts, excepted, excepting, exceptable, exception, exceptions, exceptionable, exceptionably, exceptional, exceptionally

excess excesses, excessive, excessively, excessiveness

exchange exchanges, exchanged, exchanging, exchangeable, exchanger, exchangers

excite excites, excited, exciting, excitingly, excitable, excitably, excitedly, excitement

exclaim exclaims, exclaimed, exclaiming, exclamation, exclamations, exclamatory

exclude excludes, excluded, excluding, excludable, exclusive, exclusively, exclusion, exclusiveness

excursion excursions, excursioned, excursioning, excursionist

excuse excuses, excused, excusing, excusable

execute executes, executed, executing, executor, executors, execution, executions, executioner, executioners

executive executives

exercise exercises, exercised, exercising, exerciser

exhaust exhausts, exhausted, exhausting, exhaustible, exhaustive, exhaustively, exhaustion

exhibit exhibits, exhibited, exhibiting, exhibition, exhibitions, exhibitor, exhibitors

exile exiles, exiled, exiling

exist exists, existed, existing, existence, existences, existent

expect expects, expected, expecting, expectable, expectancy, expectant, expectantly, expectation, expectedly

expedite expedites, expedited, expediting, expeditionary, expeditious, expediter

expense expenses, expensive, expensively, expensiveness

experience experiences, experienced, experiencing, experiential, experientially

experiment experiments, experimented, experimenting, experimental, experimentation

expert experts, expertly, expertness

explain explains, explained, explaining, explainable, explanatory, explanatorily, explanation, explanations

explode explodes, exploded, exploding, explosion, explosive, explosives

explore explores, explored, exploring, explorer, explorers, exploration, exploratory

export exports, exported, exporting, exportation, exporter, exporters

expose exposes, exposed, exposing, exposure, exposures, exposition

express expresses, expressed, expressing, expression, expressions, expressionless, expressive, expressively, expressiveness

exquisite exquisitely, exquisiteness

extend extends, extended, extending, extensive, extensively, extension, extensions, extender, extenders

extent extents

external externally, externalize, externalizes, externalized, externalizing

extinct extinctive, extinction

extra extras

extraordinary extraordinarily

extravagance extravagances, extravagant, extravagantly, extravagancy, extravaganza

extreme extremes, extremely, extremeness, extremism, extremist, extremity

eye

eye   eyes, eyed, eyeing, eyeless

F

face faces, faced, facing, faceless

facile facilely, facilitate, facilitates, facilitated, facilitating, facilitation, facility, facilities

fact facts, factual, factually

factory factories

faculty faculties

fade fades, faded, fading

fail fails, failed, failing, failingly, failure, failures

faint faints, fainted, fainting, fainter, faintest, faintly

fair fairs, fairer, fairest, fairly, fairness

fall falls, fell, fallen, falling

false falsely, falsify, falsified, falsifying, falsehood

falter falters, faltered, faltering, falteringly

fame famed

familiar familiarly, familiarize, familiarizes, familiarized, familiarizing, familiarity, familiarities

family families

famous famously

fan fans, fanned, fanning

fancy fancies, fancied, fancying, fancier, fanciest, fanciful, fancifully

fantasy　fantasies, fantastic, fantastical, fantastically, fantasize, fantasizes, fantasized, fantasizing, fantasia

far　farther, farthest

fare　fares, fared, faring, farewell, farewells

farm　farms, farmed, farming, farmer, farmers

fascinate　fascinates, fascinated, fascinating, fascination, fascinations

fashion　fashions, fashioned, fashioning, fashionable, fashionably

fast　faster, fastest, fasten, fastens, fastened, fastening, fastener, fasteners

fat　fats, fatter, fattest, fattened, fattening, fatty

fatal　fatality, fatalities, fatally

fate　fates, fated, fateful

father　fathers

fault　faults, faulted, faulting, faultiness, faultless, faultlessly, faulty

fatigue　fatigues, fatigued, fatiguing, fatigable

favor　favors, favored, favoring, favorite, favorites, favorable, favorably, favorableness, favoritism

fear　fears, feared, fearing, fearful, fearfully, fearfulness, fearless, fearlessly, fearlessness

feast　feasts, feasted, feasting

feather   feathers, feathered, feathering, feathery

feature   features, featured, featuring

February   Feb.

federate   federates, federated, federating, federation, federations, federal, federally, federalist

feeble   feebler, feeblest, feebly, feebleness

feed   feeds, fed, feeding, feeder, feeders

feedback

feel   feels, felt, feeling, feelings

fence   fences, fenced, fencing, fencer, fencers

festive   festival, festivals, festively, festivity

fever   fevers, feverish

few   fewer, fewest

fiber   fibers, fibered, fibrous

field   fields

fiend   fiendish, fiendishly, fiendishness

fierce   fiercer, fiercest, fiercely, fierceness

fight   fights, fought, fighting, fighter, fighters

figure   figures, figured, figuring, figurine, figurines

file   files, filed, filing, filer, filers

fill   fills, filled, filling, filler, fillers

film   films, filmed, filming, filmy

final   finals, finalize, finalizes, finalized, finalizing, finally, finale, finales, finalist, finalists, finality

finance   finances, financed, financing, financial, financials, financially, financer, financers

find   finds, found, finding

fine   fines, fined, fining, finer, finest

finger   fingers, fingered, fingering

finish   finishes, finished, finishing

fir   firs

fire   fires, fired, firing, fiery

fireplace   fireplaces

firm   firms, firmed, firming, firmer, firmest, firmly, firmness

first   firstly

fish   fishes, fished, fishing, fishy, fishery

fit   fits, fitted, fitting, fitness

five   fives, fifth, fifths

fifteen   fifteenth, fifteenths

fifty   fifties, fiftieth

fix   fixes, fixed, fixing

flag   flags, flagged, flagging

flame   flames, flamed, flaming

flash   flashes, flashed, flashing, flashy, flasher, flashers

flashlight   flashlights

flat flatten, flatter, flattest

flavor flavors, flavored, flavoring, flavorful, flavorfully, flavorsome, flavorless, flavorlessly

fleck flecks, flecked, flecking

flee flees, fled, fleeing

flick flicks, flicker, flickers, flickered, flickering

flight flights

flinch flinches, flinched, flinching

flock flocks, flocked, flocking

flood floods, flooded, flooding

floor floors

flounder flounders, floundered, floundering

flour flours, floured, flouring, floury

flourish flourishes, flourished, flourishing

flow flows, flowed, flowing

flower flowers, flowered, flowering

flu influenza

flurry flurries, flurried, flurrying

flutter flutters, fluttered, fluttering, fluttery, flutterer

fly flies, flew, flown, flying, flier, flyer, flyers

fold folds, folded, folding, folder, folders

foliage foliages, foliaged, foliate

follow

follow follows, followed, following, follower, followers

fond fonder, fondest, fondly, fondness

food foods

fool fools, fooled, fooling, foolish, foolishly, foolishness

foot feet

football footballs

for forever

forbid forbids, forbidden, forbade, forbidding, forbiddance, forbiddingly

force forces, forced, forcing, forceful, forcefully, forcible, forcibly, forcefulness

forehead foreheads

foreign foreigner, foreigners, foreignness

forest forests, forested, forestry, forester, foresters

forfeit forfeits, forfeited, forfeiting, forfeitable, forfeiter, forfeiters

forget forgets, forgot, forgetting, forgetful, forgotten

fork forks, forked, forking

form forms, formed, forming, formerly, former

formal formals, formally, formality, formalize, formation, formations

fort forts, fortress

fortify   fortifies, fortified, fortifying, fortifier, fortification, fortifications

fortune   fortunes, fortunate, fortunately, fortuneless

forward   forwards, forwarded, forwarding, forwardness

foul   fouls, fouled, fouling, foulest

fountain   fountains

four   fours, fourth, fourths

fourteen   fourteens, fourteenth

forty   forties, fortieth

fox   foxes, foxy

fracture   fractures, fractured, fracturing

fragile   fragilely, fragility, fragilities

fragment   fragments, fragmented, fragmenting, fragmentary, fragmentation

fragrance   fragrant, fragrantly

frail   frailer, frailest, frailly, frailness, frailty

frame   frames, framed, framing, framer, framers

frank   franker, frankest, frankly, frankness

freckle   freckles, freckled, freckling

free   frees, freed, freeing, freer, freest, freely, freedom, freedoms

freeze   freezes, froze, freezing, frozen, freezer, freezers

freight   freighter, freighters

frequent   frequents, frequented, frequenting, frequently, frequence, frequency, frequenter, frequentness

fresh   fresher, freshest, freshly, freshness

Friday   Fri.

friend   friends, friendly, friendlier, friendliest, friendliness, friendless, friendship, friendships

fright   frights, frighten, frightens, frightened, frightening, frighteningly, frightful, frightfully

frog   frogs

from

front   fronts, fronting

frontier   frontiers

frost   frosts, frosted, frosting, frosty

fry   fries, fried, frying

fugitive   fugitives, fugitively

full   fuller, fullest, fully, fullness

fun   funnier, funniest, funny, funnies

function   functions, functioned, functioning, functional, functionally, functionary, functionaries

fundamental   fundamentally, fundamentalist, fundamentalists

funeral   funerals, funereal

fur   furs, furry

furnace   furnaces

furnish   furnishes, furnished, furnishing, furnishings, furnisher, furniture

further   furthers, furthered, furthering, furthest, furthermore

fury   furious, furiously, furor

future   futures, futuristic

G

gain gains, gained, gaining, gainful, gainfully

gallery galleries

gallon gallons

gallop gallops, galloped, galloping, galloper

game games, gaming

gang gangs, ganged, ganging

garage garages, garaged, garaging

garbage

garden gardens, gardened, gardening, gardener

gas gases

gasoline

gate gates

gather gathers, gathered, gathering, gatherings, gatherer

gear gears, geared, gearing

general generals, generalize, generalizes, generalized, generalizing, generalist, generality, generalities, generalization, generally

generate generates, generated, generating, generation, generations, generator

generosity generous, generously

genius geniuses

gentle gentler, gentlest, gently, gentleness

genuine genuinely, genuineness

geography geographies, geographic, geographical, geographer, geographers

germ germs, germy

gesture gestures, gestured, gesturing, gesturer

get gets, got, getting, gotten

ghost ghosts, ghostly

giant giants, giantness

gift gifts, gifted

gigantic gigantically

gimmick gimmicks, gimmicky, gimmickry

girl girls

give gives, gave, given, giving, giver

glad gladder, gladdest, gladly, gladness

glance glances, glanced, glancing

glare glares, glared, glaring, glaringly

glass glasses, glassy, glassful

glimmer glimmers, glimmered, glimmering

glimpse glimpses, glimpsed, glimpsing

glitter glitters, glittered, glittering, glitteringly, glittery

globe globes, global

gloom gloomy, gloomier, gloomiest, gloomily, gloominess

glory   glories, gloried, glorying, glorify, glorifies, glorified, glorifying, glorifier, glorious, gloriously, gloriousness, glorification

glove   gloves

glow   glows, glowed, glowing

go   goes, went, going, gone

goat   goats

gold   golds, golden

golf   golfs, golfing, golfer

good   goodness

good-bye   good-byes

goose   geese

gopher   gophers

gorgeous   gorgeously, gorgeousness

gossip   gossips, gossiped, gossiping, gossipy, gossiper

govern   governs, governed, governing, governor, governors, government, governments, governess, governable

gown   gowns

grab   grabs, grabbed, grabbing

grace   graces, graced, gracing, graceful, gracefully, gracefulness, gracious, graciousness, graceless, gracelessly

grade   grades, graded, grading, grader

gradual   gradually, gradualness

graduate   graduates, graduated, graduating, graduation, graduations

grain grains, grainy

grammar grammarian, grammatical, grammatically

grand grander, grandest, grandness, grandly

grandfather grandfathers

grandmother grandmothers

grape grapes

grapefruit grapefruits

grasp grasps, grasped, grasping

grass grasses, grassy

grateful gratefully, gratefulness

gratify gratifies, gratified, gratifying, gratifier, gratitude

gravel gravels, graveled, graveling, gravelly

gray grayer, grayest

graze grazes, grazed, grazing

grease greases, greased, greasing, greasy, greasier, greasiest, greasiness

great greater, greatest, greatly, greatness

green greener, greenest

greet greets, greeted, greeting, greeter

grief grieve, grieves, grieved, grieving, grievingly, grievous, grievously, grievance, griever

grim grimmer, grimmest, grimly

grind grinds, grinding, grinder

grip   grips, gripped, gripping

groan   groans, groaned, groaning

grocery   groceries, grocer

groove   grooves, grooved, grooving, groovy

gross   grosses, grossly, grossness

ground   grounds, grounded

group   groups, grouped, grouping

grow   grows, grew, growing, grown, growth, growths, grower, growers

growl   growls, growled, growling, growler

gruff   gruffly, gruffness

guarantee   guarantees, guaranteed, guaranteeing, guaranty

guard   guards, guarded, guarding, guardedly, guardingly

guardian   guardians, guardianship

guess   guesses, guessed, guessing, guesser

guide   guides, guided, guiding, guider, guidance

gulf   gulfs

gush   gushes, gushed, gushing

gymnasium   gymnasiums, gymnast, gymnastic, gymnastics, gym

H

habit   habits

hair   hairs, hairy, hairless

half   halves

hall   halls

Halloween

hammer   hammers, hammered, hammering

hand   hands, handful, handfuls

handkerchief   handkerchiefs

handle   handles, handled, handling, handler

handsome   handsomer, handsomest, handsomely, handsomeness

handy   handier, handiest, handily, handiness

hang   hangs, hanged, hung, hanging, hanger

happen   happens, happened, happening

happy   happier, happiest, happily, happiness

harbor   harbors, harbored, harboring

hard   harder, hardest, hardly

hardware   hardwares

harm   harms, harmed, harming, harmful, harmless, harmlessness

harmony   harmonize, harmonizes, harmonized, harmonizing, harmonies, harmonious, harmoniously, harmoniousness, harmonics, harmonist

harry   harries, harried, harrying

harvest   harvests, harvested, harvesting, harvester

haste   hastens, hasten, hastened, hastening, hasty, hastily

hat   hats

hatch   hatches, hatched, hatching, hatchery

hate   hates, hated, hating, hateful, hatefully

haunt   haunts, haunted, haunting, hauntingly

have   has, had, having, hasn't, hadn't

he   he's, him, his

head   heads, headed, heading

headache   headaches

headquarters

heal   healer, healers

health   healthy, healthier, healthiest, healthful, healthfully, healthily, healthiness, healthfulness

heap   heaps, heaped, heaping

hear   hears, heard, hearing

heart   hearts

hearty   heartier, heartiest

heat   heats, heated, heating, heater

heavy   heavier, heaviest, heavily, heaviness

hedge   hedges, hedged, hedging

heel   heels, heeled, heeling

height   heights, heighten, heightens, heightened, heightening

helicopter helicopters

hello hellos

helmet helmets, helmeted

help helps, helped, helping, helpful, helpfully, helpfulness, helpless, helper

hen hens

her

herd herds, herded, herder, herding

here

hermit hermits, hermetic, hermitage

hero heroes, heroic, heroism

herself

hesitate hesitates, hesitated, hesitating, hesitatingly, hesitant, hesitater, hesitation

hide hides, hid, hiding, hidden

high higher, highest, highly, highness

highway highways

hike hikes, hiked, hiking, hiker

hill hills, hilly

him

himself

hinder hinders, hindered, hindering, hindrance

hindsight

hinge hinges, hinged, hinging

hire hires, hired, hiring

history histories, historic, historical, historically, historian

hit hits, hitting, hitter

hitch hitches, hitched, hitching

hobby hobbies, hobbyist

hold holds, held, holding, holdings, holder, holders

hole holes, holey

holiday holidays

home homes

homesick homesickness

honest honestly, honesty

honey honeys, honeyed

honor honors, honored, honoring, honorable, honorably, honorarily, honorary

hook hooks, hooked, hooking

hop hops, hopped, hopping

hope hopes, hoped, hoping, hopeful, hopefully, hopefulness, hopeless, hopelessly, hopelessness

horizon horizons

horizontal horizontally

horn horns

horror horrors, horrible, horribly, horribleness, horrify, horrifies, horrified, horrifying, horrifyingly, horrid, horridly, horridness

horse horses

horseback

hose hoses, hosed, hosing

hostile hostilely, hostility, hostilities

hot hotter, hottest

hotel hotels

hour hours, hourly, hr.

house houses

household households, householder

how

however

howl howls, howled, howling, howler

hug hugs, hugged, hugging

huge huger, hugest, hugely, hugeness

human humans, humanly, humane,
humanely, humanitarian, humanity,
humanness, humanist, humanism

humiliate humiliates, humiliated,
humiliating, humiliation, humility

humor humors, humored, humoring,
humorous, humorously, humorist,
humorists

hundred hundreds, hundredth

hunger hungers, hungered, hungering,
hungry, hungrier, hungriest, hungrily,
hungriness

hunt hunts, hunted, hunting, hunter,
hunters

hurdle hurdles, hurdled, hurdling, hurdler

hurry

hurry   hurries, hurried, hurrying
hurt   hurts, hurting, hurtful
husband husbands
hygiene hygienic, hygienically, hygienist

I

I I'd, I'll, I'm, I've

ice ices, iced, icing, icy, icicle, icicles

ice cream ice creams

idea ideas

ideal ideals, ideally, idealism, idealist, idealistic

identical identically, identicalness

idle idles, idled, idling, idly, idleness, idler

I f

ignore ignores, ignored, ignoring, ignorant, ignorantly, ignorance

ill illness

illusion illusions, illusionary, illusionist

illustrate illustrates, illustrated, illustrating, illustration, illustrative, illustrious, illustriously, illustrator

image images, imagine, imagines, imagined, imagining, imagination, imaginations, imaginative, imaginary, imagery

imitate imitates, imitated, imitating, imitation, imitative, imitator

immediate immediately, immediacy

immense immensely, immensity, immenseness

impersonate impersonates, impersonated, impersonating, impersonation, impersonator

imply   implies, implied, implying, implicit, implication

import   imports, imported, importing, importable, importer, importation

important   importantly, importance

impose   imposes, imposed, imposing, imposingly, imposer, imposition

impossible   impossibly, impossibility, impossibilities

impress   impresses, impressed, impressing, impression, impressions, impressionable, impressive, impressively, impressionism, impressionist

improbable   improbably, improbability

improve   improves, improved, improving, improvable, improvement, improvements

improvise   improvises, improvised, improvising, improviser, improvisation

impulse   impulses, impulsive, impulsively

in

inch   in., inched, inches, inching

incident   incidents, incidental, incidentally, incidence

incite   incites, incited, inciting, incitement

incline   inclines, inclined, inclining, inclination

include   includes, included, including, inclusive, inclusion

income   incomes, incoming

inconvenience inconveniences,
inconvenienced, inconveniencing,
inconvenient, inconveniently,
inconveniency

increase increases, increased, increasing,
increasingly

indeed

indefinite indefinitely, indefiniteness

independent independence, independently,
independency

Indian Indians

indicate indicates, indicated, indicating,
indicator, indication

indict indicts, indicted, indicting,
indictable, indictment

indifferent indifferently, indifference

indirect indirectly, indirection,
indirectness

individual individuals, individually,
individualist, individuality, individualize

indoor indoors

industry industries, industrial,
industrious, industriously, industrialize,
industrialism, industrialist

ineligible ineligibly, ineligibility

inevitable inevitably, inevitability

infant infants, infantile, infancy

inferior inferiority

inflame inflames, inflamed, inflaming,
inflammable, inflammatory, inflammation

inflate   inflates, inflated, inflating,
    inflatable, inflation, inflationary,
    inflationist

inflict   inflicts, inflicted, inflicting,
    inflicter, infliction

influence   influences, influenced,
    influencing, influential

inform   informs, informed, informing,
    informative, information, informational,
    informer

infrequent   infrequently, infrequence,
    infrequency, infrequentness

inhabit   inhabits, inhabited, inhabiting,
    inhabitant, inhabitants

initial   initials, initialed, initialing,
    initially

initiate   initiates, initiated, initiating,
    initiative, initiation, initiator

inject   injects, injected, injecting,
    injectable, injection, injector

injure   injures, injured, injuring,
    injurious, injuriously, injury, injuries

ink   inks, inked, inky

inning   innings

innocent   innocence, innocently

input

inquire   inquires, inquired, inquiring,
    inquiringly, inquiry, inquiries,
    inquisition, inquisitions

insect   insects, insecticide

inside   insides, insider, insiders

insist   insists, insisted, insisting, insistent, insistently

inspect   inspects, inspected, inspecting, inspection, inspections, inspector

inspire   inspires, inspired, inspiring, inspiration, inspirational

install   installs, installed, installing, installment, installation

instant   instantaneous, instantaneously, instantly, instance

instead

instinct   instincts, instinctual, instinctive, instinctively

institute   institutes, instituted, instituting, institution, institutions, institutional, institutionalize

instruct   instructs, instructed, instructing, instruction, instructions, instructional, instructive, instructively, instructor, instructors

instrument   instruments, instrumental, instrumentally, instrumentalist

insulate   insulates, insulated, insulating, insulation

insult   insults, insulted, insulting

insure   insures, insured, insuring, insurable, insurer, insurers, insurance

integrate   integrates, integrated, integrating, integrative, integration

intellect intellects, intellectual, intellectually intellectualist, intellectualize

intelligence intelligent, intelligently, intelligible, intelligibly, intelligibility

intend intends, intended, intending, intent, intention, intentions, intentional, intentionally, intently, intents

intense intensely, intenseness, intensify, intensive, intensiveness, intensively

intercept intercepts, intercepted, intercepting, interception, interceptor, interceptors

interest interests, interested, interesting, interestingly

interfere interferes, interfered, interfering, interference

interior interiors

internal internally, internalize, internalizes, internalized, internalizing, internalization

international internationally

interpret interprets, interpreted, interpreting

interrupt interrupts, interrupted, interrupting, interruption, interruptive, interrupter

interval intervals

interview interviews, interviewed, interviewing, interviewer, interviewee

intimate intimately, intimacy

into

introduce introduces, introduced, introducing, introductory, introduction, introductions

intrude intrudes, intruded, intruding, intrusive, intrusion, intruder

invade invades, invaded, invading, invasive, invasion, invasions, invader

invent invents, invented, inventing, inventive, inventively, inventiveness, invention, inventions, inventor

invest invests, invested, investing, investor, investment

investigate investigates, investigated, investigating, investigator, investigators, investigation

invisible invisibly, invisibleness

invite invites, invited, inviting, invitation, invitations

involuntary involuntarily

involve involves, involved, involving, involvement

iron irons, ironed, ironing

irony ironies, ironic, ironical, ironically

irrigate irrigates, irrigated, irrigating, irrigation

irritate irritates, irritated, irritating, irritative, irritable, irritably, irritant, irritation

island islands, islander

isolate

isolate isolates, isolated, isolating, isolation, isolationist, isolationists

issue issues, issued, issuing, issuable

it it's

item items, itemize, itemizes, itemized, itemizing, itemization

itself

J

jacket   jackets

jail   jails, jailed, jailing, jailer, jailers

January   Jan.

jar   jars, jarred, jarring

jealous   jealously, jealousy, jealousies, jealousness

jell   jells, jelled, jelling, jelly, jellies, jellied, jellying

jest   jests, jested, jesting, jester, jesters

jet   jets, jetted, jetting

jewel   jewels, jeweled, jeweling, jewelry, jeweler, jewelers

jilt   jilts, jilted, jilting

job   jobs

join   joins, joined, joining, joiner, joiners

joint   joints, jointed, jointly

joke   jokes, joked, joking, jokingly, joker, jokers

jolly   jollier, jolliest

journal   journals, journalism, journalist, journalists

journey   journeys, journeyed, journeying

joy   joyful, joyous, joyless, joyously

jubilant   jubilantly, jubilate, jubilates, jubilated, jubilating, jubilation, jubilance

judge

judge   judges, judged, judging, judgment, judgments, judgmental

juice   juices, juiced, juicing, juicy, juicier, juiciest, juiciness

July

jump   jumps, jumped, jumping, jumpy, jumpier, jumpiest

June

jungle   jungles

junior   juniors, Jr.

jury   juries, juror, jurors

just   justly, justness, justice, justify, justified, justifying, justification

K

keep keeps, kept, keeping, keeper, keepers

kettle kettles

kick kicks, kicked, kicking, kicker, kickers

kid kids, kidded, kidding, kidder, kidders

kind kinder, kindest, kindly, kindness

kindle kindles, kindled, kindling

king kings, kingly, kingdom, kingdoms

kitchen kitchens

kite kites

kitten kittens, kitty, kitties

knee knees, kneel, kneels, knelt, kneeled, kneeling

knife knifes, knifed, knifing, knives

knight knights, knighted, knighting, knightly

knit knits, knitted, knitting, knitter, knitters

knock knocks, knocked, knocking, knocker

knot knots, knotted, knotting, knotty

know knows, knew, known, knowing, knowingly, knowledge, knowledgeable, knowledgeably

L

labor labors, labored, laboring, laborious, laboriously, laborer, laborers

laboratory laboratories, lab, labs

lace laces, laced, lacing, lacy

ladder ladders

lady ladies

lake lakes

lamb lambs

lamp lamps

land lands, landed, landing, landings

landlord landlords

landscape landscapes, landscaped, landscaping, landscaper, landscapers

landslide landslides

language languages

lantern lanterns

large larger, largest, largely, largeness

last lasts, lasted, lasting, lastingly, lastly, lastingness

late later, latest, lately, lateness

latter latterly

laugh laughs, laughed, laughing, laughable, laughter

launch launches, launched, launching, launcher, launchers

laundry laundries, launder, launders, laundered, laundering, launderer, laundromat

law laws, lawful, lawless, lawyer, lawyers

lawn lawns

lay lays, laid, lain, laying

lazy lazier, laziest, lazily, laziness

lead leads, led, leading, leader, leaders

leaf leaves, leafy

league leagues

leak leaks, leaked, leaking, leaky

lean leans, leaned, leaning, leaner, leanest

learn learns, learned, learning, learner, learners

lease leases, leased, leasing

leash leashes, leashed, leashing

leather leathers, leathered, leathery

leave leaves, left, leaving

leeway leeways

leg legs

legal legally, legality, legalize, legalizes, legalized, legalizing, legalization

legion legions, legionary, legionnaire, legionnaires

legislate legislates, legislated, legislating, legislator, legislators, legislature, legislatures, legislation, legislative

leisure leisurely, leisureliness

lemon   lemons, lemony

lemonade

lend   lends, lent, lending, lender, lenders

length   lengths, lengthen, lengthens, lengthened, lengthening, lengthy, lengthier, lengthiest

less   lesser, least, lessen, lessens, lessened, lessening

lesson   lessons

let   lets, letting

letter   letters, lettered, lettering

lettuce

levee   levees, leveed, leveeing

level   levels, leveled, leveling, levelness, leveler, levelers

levy   levies, levied, levying

liable   liability, liabilities

libel   libels, libeled, libeling, libelous

liberate   liberates, liberated, liberating, liberation, liberty, liberties, liberal, liberator, liberators

library   libraries, librarian, librarians

license   licenses, licensed, licensing

lie   lies, lied, lying, liar, liars, lay, lain

lieutenant   lieutenants

life   lifeless, lifelessness

lift   lifts, lifted, lifting, lifter, lifters

light lights, lighted, lit, lighting, lightly, lighter, lightest, lightness, lighten, lightened

lightning

like likes, liked, liking, likely, likelier, likeliest, likeliness, likable, liken, likeness

limb limbs

limber limbers, limbered, limbering

limit limits, limited, limiting, limitless, limitation, limitations

limp limps, limped, limping

line lines, lined, lining, liner, liners

linen linens

linger lingers, lingered, lingering, lingerer, lingerers

lion lions, lioness

liquid liquids, liquefy, liquefies, liquefied, liquefying, liquidity, liquidness

list lists, listed, listing

listen listens, listened, listening, listener, listeners

literature literatures, literate, literately, literacy, literary, literateness

little littler, littlest

live lives, lived, living, lively, livelier, liveliest, livable

load loads, loaded, loading, loader, loaders

loaf loafs, loafed, loafing, loafer, loafers

loan loans, loaned, loaning

local locally, localize, localizes, localized, localizing, locale, locales, locality, localities, localization

locate locates, located, locating, location, locations

lock locks, locked, locking

lodge lodges, lodged, lodging, lodger, lodgers

log logs, logging, logger, loggers

logic logical, logically, logicalness, logician

loiter loiters, loitered, loitering, loiterer, loiterers

lone lonely, lonelier, loneliest, lonesome, loner, loners, loneliness

long longer, longest

look looks, looked, looking, looker, lookers

loop loops, looped, looping

loose loosen, loosens, loosened, loosening, looser, loosest, loosely, looseness

lose loses, lost, losing, loser, losers, loss, losses

lot lots

loud louder, loudest, loudly, loudness

love loves, loved, loving, lovable, lovely, lovelier, loveliest, loveliness

low lower, lowest

loyal loyally, loyalty, loyalties, loyalism, loyalist

luck lucky, luckier, luckiest, luckily

lump lumps, lumped, lumping, lumpy, lumpier, lumpiest, lumpiness

lunch lunches, lunched, lunching, luncheon, luncheons

lung lungs

lunge lunges, lunged, lunging, lunger, lungers

luscious lusciously, lusciousness

luster lusters, lustered, lustering, lustrous, lustrously

luxury luxuries, luxurious, luxuriously, luxuriant

lyric lyrics, lyrical, lyricism, lyricist, lyricists

M

machine machines, machinery, machinist, machinists

mad madder, maddest, madden, maddens, maddened, maddening, madly, madness

magazine magazines

magic magical, magically, magician, magicians

magnificence magnificent, magnificently

mail mails, mailed, mailing, mailer, mailers

maintain maintains, maintained, maintaining, maintainable, maintenance

majesty majesties, majestic, majestical, majestically

major majors, majored, majoring, majority, majorities

make makes, made, making

malfunction malfunctions, malfunctioned, malfunctioning

mammal mammals

man men

manage manages, managed, managing, manageable, manager, managers, management

maneuver maneuvers, maneuvered, maneuvering, maneuverable, maneuverability

manipulate   manipulates, manipulated,
   manipulating, manipulative,
   manipulatory, manipulation,
   manipulator, manipulators

manner   manners, mannered, mannerly,
   mannerism, mannerisms

mansion   mansions

manual   manuals, manually

manufacture   manufactures, manufactured,
   manufacturing, manufacturer,
   manufacturers

many

map   maps, mapped, mapping

marathon   marathon, marathoner,
   marathoners

marble   marbles, marbled, marbling

March   Mar.

margin   margins, margined, margining,
   marginal, marginally

mark   marks, marked, marking, marker,
   markers

marry   marries, married, marrying,
   marriage, marriages

marvel   marvels, marveled, marveling,
   marvelous, marvelously

mascot   mascots

mask   masks, masked, masking

mass   masses, massed, massing, massive,
   massively, massiveness

massage massages, massaged, massaging, massager, massagers

master masters, mastered, mastering, masterful, masterfully, masterly, mastery

mat mats, matted, matting

match matches, matched, matching, matchless

material materials, materialize, materializes, materialized, materializing

maternal maternally, maternity

mathematics mathematical, mathematically, mathematician, mathematicians, math

matter matters, mattered

mature matures, matured, maturing, maturely, maturate, maturation

May

maybe may

mayor mayors, mayoral

me

meadow meadows

meal meals

mean means, meant, meaning, meaningful, meaningless, meaner, meanest, meanly, meanness

meantime

meanwhile

measure measures, measured, measuring, measurable, measurably, measurement, measurements

meat meats, meaty, meatier, meatiest

mechanize mechanizes, mechanized, mechanizing, mechanization mechanism, mechanisms, mechanic, mechanics, mechanical, mechanically

medal medals, medalist, medallion, medallions

medicine medicines, medicinal, medical, medically, medicate, medicates, medicated, medicating, medication, medications, medic, medics

medium mediums, media, median

meet meets, met, meeting

melt melts, melted, melting

member members, membership, memberships

membrane membranes, membraned, membranous

memory memories, memorize, memorizes, memorized, memorizing, memorization, memorable, memorably, memorial, memorials, memorialize, memorabilia, memoir, memoirs

memorandum memoranda, memo, memos

mention mentions, mentioned, mentioning, mentionable

merchant merchants, merchandise, merchandises, merchandised, merchandising, merchandiser

mere   merest, merely

merit   merits, merited, meriting, meritorious

merry   merrier, merriest, merrily, merriness

message   messages, messenger, messengers

metal   metals, metallic

meter   meters, metered, metering, metric, metrics, metrical, metrically

method   methods

metropolis   metropolitan

middle   mid, midst

midnight   midnights

might   mighty, mightier, mightiest, mightily, mightiness

migrate   migrates, migrated, migrating, migratory, migration, migrant, migrants, migrator, migrators

mild   milder, mildest, mildly, mildness

mile   miles, mileage

milk   milks, milked, milking, milky

mill   mills, miller, millers

million   millions, millionth, millionaire, millionaires

mimic   mimics, mimicked, mimicking, mimicry

mind   minds, minded, minding

mine   mines, mined, mining, miner, miners

mineral   minerals, mineralize,
   mineralizes, mineralized, mineralizing,
   mineralogy, mineralogist, mineralogists

minimum   minimums, minimal, minimize

minor   minors, minored, minoring,
   minority, minorities

mint   mints, minted, minting, minty

minute   minutes, min., mins.

mirror   mirrors, mirrored, mirroring

miscalculate   miscalculates, miscalculated,
   miscalculating, miscalculation,
   miscalculations

mischief   mischievous, mischievously

misery   miseries, miserable, miserably,
   miserableness

misinterpret   misinterprets,
   misinterpreted, misinterpreting,
   misinterpretation, misinterpretations

miss   misses, missed, missing

misspell   misspells, misspelled,
   misspelling, misspeller, misspellers

mist   mists, misted, misting, misty

mistake   mistakes, mistook, mistaking,
   mistaken, mistakenly, mistakable

misuse   misuses, misused, misusing,
   misusage

mix   mixes, mixed, mixing, mixer, mixers,
   mixture, mixtures

model   models, modeled, modeling

modest   modestly, modesty

modify   modifies, modified, modifying, modifiable, modification, modifications, modifier, modifiers

moist   moisten, moistens, moistened, moistening, moisture, moistness, moisturize, moisturizes, moisturized, moisturizing

molten

mom   moms, mommy

moment   moments, momentary, momentous, momentarily

Monday   Mon.

money   moneys, monies

monkey   monkeys

monopoly   monopolies, monopolize, monopolizes, monopolized, monopolizing, monopolist, monopolists, monopolistic, monopolizer, monopolizers

monster   monsters, monstrous, monstrously, monstrosity, monstrosities

month   months, monthly, bimonthly

monument   monuments, monumental, monumentally

mood   moods, moody, moodier, moodiest, moodily, moodiness

moon   moons

moral   morals, moralistic, moralistically, morally, moralize, moralizes, moralized, moralizing, moralism, morale, morality, moralist, moralists

more   most, mostly

morning   mornings

mortal   mortally, mortality

mortgage   mortgages, mortgaged,
   mortgaging, mortgagee, mortgagees,
   mortgager, mortgagers

mosquito   mosquitoes

moss   mosses, mossy

mother   mothers

motion   motions, motioned, motioning,
   motionless

motive   motives, motivate, motivates,
   motivated, motivating, motivation,
   motivator, motivators

motor   motors, motored, motoring,
   motorize, motorist, motorists

motto   mottos

mount   mounts, mounted, mounting

mountain   mountains, mountainous,
   mountaineer, mountaineers, mountainside

mourn   mourns, mourned, mourning,
   mournful, mournfully, mourner,
   mourners

mouse   mice, mousy

mouth   mouths, mouthful

move   moves, moved, moving, movable,
   mover, movers, movement

movie   movies

much

mud

mud muddy, muddies, muddied, muddying, muddier, muddiest, muddiness

multiply multiplies, multiplied, multiplying, multiple, multiples, multiplication, multiplier, multipliers

multitude multitudes, multitudinous

mural murals

murmur murmurs, murmured, murmuring

muscle muscles, muscled, muscling, muscular

museum museums

music musical, musicals, musically, musician, musicians

must

mustard mustards

mutilate mutilates, mutilated, mutilating, mutilation, mutilator, mutilators

my

myself

mystery mysteries, mysterious, mysteriously

mystify mystifies, mystified, mystifying, mystification

N

nail   nails, nailed, nailing

name   names, named, naming, namely

nap   naps, napped, napping

narrate   narrates, narrated, narrating, narrative, narratives, narration, narrations, narrator, narrators

nation   nations, national, nationally, nationalist, nationality, nationalities

natural   naturally, naturalistic, naturalness, naturalize, naturalized, naturalizing, naturalist, naturalists

nature   natures, natured

naughty   naughtier, naughtiest, naughtily, naughtiness

navy   navies, naval

near   nears, neared, nearing, nearer, nearest, nearness, nearly

nearby

neat   neater, neatest, neatly, neatness

necessary   necessarily, necessitate, necessitates, necessitated, necessitating, necessity, necessities

neck   necks

necktie   neckties

need   needs, needed, needing, needy, needier, neediest, needless, needlessly, needlessness

needle needles, needled, needling, needler, needlers

neglect neglects, neglected, neglecting, neglectful, neglectfully, negligent, negligence, negligible

neighbor neighbors, neighboring, neighborliness, neighborly, neighborhood, neighborhoods

neither

nephew nephews

nerve nerves, nerved, nerving, nervous, nervously, nervousness, nervy, nervier, nerviest

nest nests, nesting, nester, nesters

net nets, netting

never

new newer, newest, newly

newsletter newsletters

newspaper newspapers

next

nice nicer, nicest, nicely

nickel nickels

niece nieces

night nights, nightly

nine nines, ninth, ninths

nineteen nineteens, nineteenth

no none, not, nothing

noble   nobler, noblest, nobly, nobles, nobility, nobleness

nobody

noise   noises, noisy, noisier, noisiest, noisily, noisiness

nonsense   nonsensical, nonsensically

noodle   noodles

noon   noons

normal   normally, normalize, normalized, normalizing, normalcy, normality

north   northerly, northern, northerner, northward

nose   noses, nosy

note   notes, noted, noting, notable, notably, notate, notates, notated, notating, notation, notations

notebook   notebooks

notice   notices, noticed, noticing, noticeable, noticeably, notify, notifies, notified, notifying

notorious   notoriously, notoriety

novel   novels, novelize, novelist, novelists

novelty   novelties

November   Nov.

now

nowhere

nuisance   nuisances

numb   numbs, numbed, numbing, numbly

number

number   numbers, numbered, numbering

numeral   numerals, numerate, numerates, numerated, numerating, numeration, numerator, numerators, numeric, numerical, numerically, numerous

nurse   nurses, nursed, nursing, nursery

nut   nuts, nutty

O

o'clock

oak oaks

obey obeys, obeyed, obeying, obedient, obedience, obediently

object objects, objected, objecting, objection, objectionable, objectionably

obligate obligates, obligated, obligating, obligatory, obligation, obligations

oblige obliges, obliged, obliging

observe observes, observed, observing, observation, observations, observational, observable, observatory, observatories, observant, observer, observers

obtain obtains, obtained, obtaining, obtainable, obtainment

obvious obviously, obviousness

occasion occasions, occasioned, occasioning, occasional, occasionally

occupy occupies, occupied, occupying, occupant, occupants, occupation, occupations, occupational

occur occurs, occurred, occurring, occurrence, occurrences

ocean oceans

October Oct.

odd odds, odder, oddest, oddly, oddity, oddness

odor odors, odorous

of

of

off

offend offends, offended, offending, offender, offenders

offense offenses, offensive, offensively, offensiveness

offer offers, offered, offering

office offices, official, officials, officially, officiate, officer, officers, officiary

often oftener, oftenest

oh

oil oils, oiled, oiling, oily, oiler, oilers

old older, oldest, oldster, oldsters

omit omits, omitted, omitting, omisive, omissible, omission, omissions

on

once

one

onion onions

only

open opens, opened, opening, openings, opener, openers, openly

opera operas, operetta, operettas, operatic

operate operates, operated, operating, operation, operations, operational, operator, operators

opinion opinions, opinionated

opportunity opportunities, opportunist, opportunists, opportunistic, opportune, opportunely, opportunism

oppose opposes, opposed, opposing, opposite, opposites, oppositely, opposition, oppositeness

optimism optimistic, optimistically, optimist, optimists

option options, optioned, optional, optionally

or

orange oranges

orbit orbits, orbited, orbiting, orbital, orbiter, orbiters

orchard orchards

orchestra orchestras, orchestrate, orchestrates, orchestrated, orchestrating, orchestration, orchestrations

order orders, ordered, ordering, orderly, orderlies

ordinary ordinarily, ordinariness

ore ores

organ organs, organist, organists

organic organism, organisms, organically

organize organizes, organized, organizing, organizer, organizers, organization, organizations

origin origins, original, originals, originally, originate, originates, originality, originator, originators

ornament   ornaments, ornamented,
   ornamenting, ornamental, ornamentally,
   ornamentation, ornamentations

other   others, otherwise

ought

ounce   ounces, oz.

our   ours, ourselves

out   outs

outdoor   outdoors

outfit   outfits, outfitted, outfitting,
   outfitter, outfitters

outline   outlines, outlined, outlining

outside   outsides, outsider, outsiders

oval   ovals

over

overcome   overcomes, overcame,
   overcoming

overflow   overflows, overflowed,
   overflowing, overflowingly

oversight   oversights

overture   overtures

overturn   overturns, overturned,
   overturning

owe   owes, owed, owing

owl   owls, owlish, owlet, owlets

own   owns, owned, owning, owner, owners,
   ownership

oyster   oysters

P

pack packs, packed, packing, packer, packers

package packages, packaged, packaging

paddle paddles, paddled, paddling

page pages, paged, paging, paginate, pagination

pageant pageants, pageantry, pageantries

pail pails

pain pains, pained, painful, painfully, painfulness, painless, painlessly, painlessness

paint paints, painted, painting, painter, painters

pair pairs, paired, pairing

pajamas

palace palaces

palm palms, palmed, palming, palmist, palmists, palmistry

pamphlet pamphlets, pamphleteer, pamphleteers

pan pans, panned, panning

pants

paper papers, papered, papering

parade parades, paraded, parading

paradise paradises

paragraph paragraphs, paragraphed, paragraphing

parallel   parallels, paralleled, parralleling

parcel   parcels, parceled, parceling

pardon   pardons, pardoned, pardoning,
  pardonable

parent   parents, parental

park   parks, parked, parking

part   parts, parted, parting, partly, partial,
  partially

participate   participates, participated,
  participating, participation, participant,
  participants

particular   particulars, particularly,
  particularity

partner   partners, partnership

party   parties, partied, partying, partyer,
  partyers

pass   passes, passed, passing, passer,
  passers

passage   passages, passaged, passaging,
  passenger, passengers

past   pasts

paste   pastes, pasted, pasting, pasty

pasture   pastures, pastured, pasturing

pat   pats, patted, patting

patch   patches, patched, patching

patent   patents, patented, patenting

path   paths

pathway   pathways

patience   patient, patients, patiently

pattern   patterns, patterned, patterning

pause pauses, paused, pausing

pave paves, paved, paving, pavement, pavements

pay pays, paid, paying, payable, payment, payments

peace peaceful, peacefully, peacefulness

peanut peanuts

peculiar   peculiarly, peculiarity, peculiarities

peek peeks, peeked, peeking

peer   peers, peered, peering

pen pens, penned, penning

pencil   pencils, penciled, penciling

pennant pennants

penny pennies, penniless

people   peoples, peopled, peopling

percent   percents, percentage, percentages, percentile, percentiles

perfect   perfects, perfected, perfecting, perfectly, perfectness, perfection, perfectionist

perform   performs, performed, performing, performance, performances, performer, performers

perfume   perfumes, perfumed, perfumer, perfumers, perfumery, perfumeries

perhaps

peril   perils, periled, periling, perilous, perilously

period   periods, periodical, periodicals, periodically

perish   perishes, perished, perishing, perishable, perishables

permanent   permanently, permanence, permanency

permit   permits, permitted, permitting, permission, permissions, permissible, permissive, permissively, permissiveness

persevere   perseveres, persevered, persevering, perseverance

persist   persists, persisted, persisting, persistent, persistently, persistence, persistency

person   persons, personal, personally, personable, personalize, personality, personalities

persuade   persuades, persuaded, persuading, persuasive, persuasively, persuasiveness, persuasion, persuasions, persuader, persuaders

pet   pets

petition   petitions, petitioned, petitioning, petitioner, petitioners

petrify   petrifies, petrified, petrifying, petrification

phone   phones, phoned, phoning

photograph photographs, photographed, photographing, photo, photography, photographer, photographers

phrase phrases, phrased, phrasing

physical physically

physician physicians

physics physicist, physicists

piano pianos, pianist, pianists

pick picks, picked, picking, picky, picker, pickers

pickle pickles, pickled, pickling

picnic picnics, picnicked, picnicking, picnicker, picnickers

picture pictures, pictured, picturing

pie pies

piece pieces, pieced, piecing

pier piers

pierce pierces, pierced, piercing, piercingly

pig pigs, piglet, piglets

pigeon pigeons

pile piles, piled, piling

pilgrim pilgrims, pilgrimage, pilgrimages

pillow pillows, pillowed, pillowing

pin pins, pinned, pinning

pink pinker, pinkest

pitch pitches, pitched, pitching, pitcher, pitchers

pity   pities, pitied, pitying, pityingly,
    pitiful, pitifully, piteous, piteously

pivot   pivots, pivoted, pivoting, pivotal,
    pivotally

place   places, placed, placing, placement,
    placements

plain   plains, plainer, plainest, plainly,
    plainness

plan   plans, planned, planning, planner,
    planners

plane   planes, planed, planing

planet   planets, planetary, planetarium,
    planetariums

plank   planks, planked, planking

plant   plants, planted, planting, planter,
    planters, plantation, plantations

plaster   plasters, plastered, plastering,
    plasterer, plasterers

plastic   plastics

platform   platforms

play   plays, played, playing, playful,
    playfully, playfulness, player, players

playground   playgrounds

playmate   playmates

pleasant   pleasantly, pleasantness,
    pleasantry, pleasantries, pleasance

please   pleases, pleased, pleasing,
    pleasingly, pleaser, pleasers

pleasure pleasures, pleasured, pleasuring, pleasurable, pleasurably, pleasureful, pleasurefully

pledge pledges, pledged, pledging, pledgee, pledgees

plenty plentiful, plentifully, plentifulness

plum plums

plunge plunges, plunged, plunging, plunger, plungers

pocket pockets, pocketed, pocketing, pocketful, pocketfuls

pocketbook pocketbooks

poem poems, poet, poets, poetry, poetries

point points, pointed, pointing, pointedly, pointless, pointer, pointers

poise poises, poised, poising

poison poisons, poisoned, poisoning, poisonous

police

policy policies

polish polishes, polished, polishing, polisher, polishers

polite politely, politeness

politics politic, politick, politicking, political, politically, politicize, politician, politicians

pollute pollutes, polluted, polluting, pollution, pollutant, pollutants, polluter

pond ponds

pony ponies

pool pools

poor poorer, poorest, poorly, poorness

popcorn

popular popularly, popularity, popularize, popularizes

porch porches

porter porters

portion portions, portioned, portioning

pose posed, posing, posable

position positions, positioned, positioning

positive positively, positiveness

possess possesses, possessed, possessing, possession, possessions, possessive, possessively, possessiveness, possessor, possessors

possible possibly, possibility, possibilities

post posts, posted, posting, postage, postal

poster posters

postpone postpones, postponed, postponing, postponement, postponements

pot pots, potted, potting

potato potatoes

potential potentially, potentiality

poultry poultries

pound pounds, pounded, pounding, poundage, poundages, lb., lbs.

pour   pours, poured, pouring, pourable

poverty   poverties

powder   powders, powdered, powdering

power   powers, powered, powering, powerful, powerfully, powerfulness, powerless, powerlessly, powerlessness

practice   practices, practiced, practicing, practical, practically, practicality, practicalness, practicable, practitioner, practitioners

prairie   prairies

praise   praises, praised, praising

preach   preaches, preached, preaching, preacher, preachers

precaution   precautions, precautionary

precious   preciously, preciousness

precise   precisely, preciseness, precision, precisionist, precisionists

predict   predicts, predicted, predicting, predictable

prefer   prefers, preferred, preferring, preferable, preferably, preferential, preference, preferences

preliminary   preliminaries, preliminarily

premature   prematurely

premium   premiums

prepare   prepares, prepared, preparing, preparedly, preparatory, preparedness, preparation, preparations

present presents, presented, presenting, presentable, presently, presentably, presentation, presentations, presenter, presenters, presence

preside presides, presided, presiding, presider, presiders

president presidents, presidential, presidency

press presses, pressed, pressing, pressingly

pressure pressures, pressured, pressuring, pressurize, pressurizes, pressurized, pressurizing

presume presumes, presumed, presuming, presumedly, presumptive, presumptous, presumption, presumptions, presumably

pretend pretends, pretended, pretending, pretender, pretenders, pretentious, pretentiously

pretty prettier, prettiest, prettily, prettiness

prevail prevails, prevailed, prevailing, prevailingly, prevailer, prevailers

prevent prevents, prevented, preventing, preventable, preventative, preventive, preventiveness, prevention, preventions

previous previously

price prices, priced, pricing, priceless, pricelessly

pride prides, prided, priding, prideful, pridefully

prim prims, primmed, primming, primmer, primmest, primly, primness

primary primaries, primarily

prime primes, primed, priming, primely, primer, primers

primitive primitives, primitively, primitivism

prince princes, princely, princess, princesses

principal principals, principality

principle principles, principled

print prints, printed, printing, printer, printers

prior priority, priorities

prison prisons, prisoner, prisoners

private privates, privately, privacy

privilege privileges, privileged

prize prizes, prized, prizing

probably probable, probability, probabilities

problem problems, problematic, problematically

procedure procedures, procedural, procedurally

proceed proceeds, proceeded, proceeding, proceedingly

process processes, processed, processing

procession processions, processional, processionals

proclaim proclaims, proclaimed, proclaiming, proclamation, proclamations

produce produces, produced, producing, producer, producers, producible

product products, productive, productively, productiveness, productivity, production, productions

profess professes, professed, professing, profession, professions, professional, professionally, professionalism, professor, professors

profit profits, profited, profiting, profitable, profitably, profitability, profitabilities

program programs, programmed, programming, programmer, programmers

progress progresses, progressed, progressing, progressive, progressively, progression, progressions

project projects, projected, projecting, projector, projectors

prominent prominently, prominence, prominences

promise promises, promised, promising, promisingly, promissory, promissories

promote promotes, promoted, promoting, promotable, promotion, promotions, promotional, promoter, promoters

prompt prompts, prompted, prompting, promptly, promptness, prompter, prompters

pronounce   pronounces, pronounced, pronouncing, pronounceable, pronounceability, pronunciation, pronunciations, pronouncement, pronouncements

proper   properly, properness

propose   proposes, proposed, proposing, proposal, proposals

propriety   proprieties

prosper   prospers, prospered, prospering, prosperity, prosperous, prosperously

protect   protects, protected, protecting, protection, protections, protective, protector, protectors

protest   protests, protested, protesting, protester, protesters, protestation, protestations

proud   prouder, proudest, proudly

prove   proves, proved, proof, proofs, proofed, proofing, proven, proving

provide   provides, provided, providing, provider, providers, provision, provisions

provoke   provokes, provoked, provoking, provocative, provocatively, provocation, provocations, provoker, provokers

prune   prunes, pruned, pruning

psychology   psychologies, psychologize, psychological, psychologically, psychologist, psychologists

public publics, publicly, publicize, publicizes, publicized, publicizing, publicity, publicist, publicists

publish publishes, published, publishing, publisher, publishers, publication, publications

pull pulls, pulled, pulling

pump pumps, pumped, pumping, pumper, pumpers

pumpkin pumpkins

punctual punctually, punctualness, punctuality

punish punishes, punished, punishing, punishable, punishment, punishments

puny punier, puniest, puniness

pupil pupils

puppy puppies, puppyish, puppyishly

purchase purchases, purchased, purchasing, purchasable

purple purples, purpled, purpling, purplish

purpose purposes, purposely, purposeful, purposefully, purposefulness, purposeless

purse purses, pursed, pursing

pursue pursues, pursued, pursuing, pursuance, pursuances, pursuer, pursuers, pursuit, pursuits

push pushes, pushed, pushing, pushiness, pushy

put   puts, putting

puzzle   puzzles, puzzled, puzzling, puzzler, puzzlers, puzzlement, puzzlements

Q

quaint   quainter, quaintest, quaintly, quaintness

qualify   qualifies, qualified, qualifying, qualification, qualifications, qualifier, qualifiers

quality   qualities

quantify   quantifies, quantified, quantifying

quantity   quantities, quantitative, quantitatively

quarrel   quarrels, quarreled, quarreling, quarrelsome, quarreler, quarrelers

quart   quarts

quarter   quarters, quartered, quartering, quarterly

queen   queens, queenly, queenlier, queenliest

quest   quests, quested, questing

question   questions, questioned, questioning, questionable, questionably, questioner, questioners, questionnaire, questionnaires

quick   quicker, quickest, quickly, quickness

quiet   quiets, quieted, quieting, quieter, quietest, quietly, quietness

quit   quits, quitted, quitting, quitter, quitters

quite

quote   quotes, quoted, quoting, quotable, quotation, quotations, quoter, quoters

R

rabbit   rabbits

race   races, raced, racing, racer, racers

rack   racks

racket   rackets, racketeers, racketeering

radiant   radiantly, radiate, radiates, radiated, radiating, radiance, radiation, radiator, radiators

radio   radios

rag   rags, ragged, raggedly, raggedness

raid   raids, raided, raiding, raider, raiders

rain   rains, rained, raining, rainy, rainier, rainiest

raise   raises, raised, raising

raisin   raisins

rake   rakes, raked, raking

rally   rallies, rallied, rallying

ranch   ranches, ranching, rancher, ranchers

random   randomly, randomness

range   ranges, ranged, ranging, ranger, rangers

rank   ranks, ranked, ranking

rapid   rapids, rapidly, rapidity, rapidness

rare   rarer, rarest, rarely, rareness, rarity, rarities

rascal   rascals, rascally

rat   rats

rate   rates, rated, rating, ratings, ratio, ratios, ration, rations

rather

ray   rays

reach   reaches, reached, reaching, reachable

read   reads, reading, readable, reader, readers

ready   readier, readiest, readiness

real   realism, realist, realistic, reality, realities

realize   realizes, realized, realizing, realization, realizations

really

reason   reasons, reasoned, reasoning, reasonable, reasonably, reasonableness

receive   receives, received, receiving, receipt, receipts, receivable, receiver, receivers, reception, receptive

recent   recently, recentness, recency

recess   recesses, recessed, recessing, recession, recessions

reckless   recklessly, recklessness

recognize   recognizes, recognized, recognizing, recognizable, recognition

recommend   recommends, recommended, recommending, recommendable, recommendation, recommendations

record   records, recorded, recording, recorder, recorders

recover   recovers, recovered, recovering, recovery, recoveries

red   redden, reddened, reddening, redder, reddest

reduce   reduces, reduced, reducing, reducible, reduction, reductions

refer   refers, referred, referring, reference, references, referenced, referencing, referral, referrals

refine   refines, refined, refining, refiner, refiners, refinement, refinements, refinery, refineries

reflect   reflects, reflected, reflection, reflections, reflector, reflectors

reflex   reflexes, reflexed, reflexing, reflexive, reflexively

reform   reforms, reformed, reforming, reformation, reformatory, reformatories, reformer, reformers

refrigerate   refrigerates, refrigerated, refrigerating, refrigeration, refrigerator, refrigerators

refuge   refuges, refuged, refuging, refugee, refugees

refuse   refuses, refused, refusing, refusal, refusals

regain   regains, regained, regaining

regard   regards, regarded, regarding, regardless, regardlessly

register

register registers, registered, registering,
registration, registrations, registrant,
registrants, registry, registrar,
registrars

regret regrets, regretted, regretting,
regretful, regretfully, regrettable

regular regularly, regularity, regulate,
regulates, regulated, regulating,
regulation, regulations

reign reigns, reigned, reigning

reinforce reinforces, reinforced,
reinforcing, reinforcement,
reinforcements

reject rejects, rejected, rejecting,
rejection, rejections

relate relates, related, relating, relation,
relations, relative, relatives, relatively

relax relaxes, relaxed, relaxing, relaxant,
relaxants, relaxation

release releases, released, releasing

relieve relieves, relieved, relieving,
relievable, reliever, relievers, relief,
reliefs

religion religions, religious, religiously,
religiousness

rely relies, relied, relying, reliable,
reliably, reliability

remain remains, remained, remaining,
remainder, remainders

remark remarks, remarked, remarking,
remarkable, remarkably

remedy remedies, remedied, remedying

remember remembers, remembered, remembering, remembrance, remembrances

remind reminds, reminded, reminding, reminder, reminders

remnant remnants

remote remoter, remotest, remotely, remoteness

remove removes, removed, removing, remover, removers, removal, removable

render renders, rendered, rendering, rendition, renditions

renew renews, renewed, renewing, renewable, renewal, renewals

rent rents, rented, renting, rental, rentals, renter, renters

repair repairs, repaired, repairing, repairer, repairers

repeat repeats, repeated, repeating, repeatable, repeatedly, repetitious, repetitiously, repetitive, repetitively, repetition, repetitions, repeater, repeaters

replace replaces, replaced, replacing, replacement, replacements

reply replies, replied, replying

report reports, reported, reporting, reporter, reporters

represent represents, represented, representing, representable, representation, representative, representatives

republic   republics, republican, republicans

request   requests, requested, requesting

require   requires, required, requiring, requirement, requirements

research   researches, researched, researching, researcher, researchers

resemble   resembles, resembled, resembling, resemblance

resent   resents, resented, resenting, resentful, resentfully, resentment, resentments

reserve   reserves, reserved, reserving, reservedly, reservation, reservations

reside   resides, resided, residing, residence, residences, residency, residencies, resident, residential

resist   resists, resisted, resisting, resistance, resistant, resistible, resister, resisters

resolve   resolves, resolved, resolving, resolvable, resolution, resolutions

resort   resorts, resorted, resorting

resource   resources, resourceful, resourcefully, resourcefulness

respect   respects, respected, respecting, respectable, respectably, respectability, respectful, respectfully

response   responses, responsible, responsibly, responsibility, responsibilities

rest   rests, rested, resting

restaurant   restaurants

restore   restores, restored, restoring,
   restorable, restoration, restorations

result   results, resulted, resulting

resume   resumes, resumed, resuming,
   resumption, resumptions

retain   retains, retained, retaining,
   retainable, retention, retainment,
   retainer, retainers

retreat   retreats, retreated, retreating

return   returns, returned, returning,
   returnable

reverse   reverses, reversed, reversing,
   reversely, reversal, reversals,
   reversible, reversibility, reversibilities

revise   revises, revised, revising, revision,
   revisions

revolt   revolts, revolted, revolting,
   revolution, revolutions, revolutionary,
   revolutionaries, revolutionist,
   revolutionize, revolutionized

revolve   revolves, revolved, revolving,
   revolvable, revolver, revolvers

reward   rewards, rewarded, rewarding

ribbon   ribbons

rice

rich   riches, richer, richest, richly,
   richness

ride   rides, rode, ridden, riding, rider,
   riders

ridicule   ridicules, ridiculed, ridiculing, ridiculous, ridiculously, ridiculousness

rifle   rifles, rifled, rifling, riflery

right   rights, righted, rightly, rightness

rigid   rigidly, rigidity, rigidness

ring   rings, rang rung, ringing

rinse   rinses, rinsed, rinsing

ripe   riper, ripest, ripen, ripens, ripened, ripening, ripeness

rise   rises, risen, rising

risk   risks, risked, risking, riskier, riskiest, risky

rival   rivals, rivaled, rivaling, rivalry, rivalries

river   rivers

road   roads

roam   roams, roamed, roaming

roar   roars, roared, roaring

robin   robins

robot   robots, robotic, robotics

rock   rocks, rocked, rocking, rocky, rockier, rockiest

roll   rolls, rolled, rolling, roller, rollers

roof   roofs, roofed, roofing, roofer, roofers

room   rooms, roomy, roomier, roomiest

rooster   roosters

root   roots, rooted, rooting

rope   ropes, roped, roping

rose   roses, rosy

rot   rots, rotted, rotting, rotten, rottener, rottenest, rottenly, rottenness

rotate   rotates, rotated, rotating, rotation, rotations, rotational, rotator, rotators, rotary, rotaries

rough   roughs, roughed, roughing, rougher, roughest, roughly, roughness

round   rounder, roundest, roundly

route   routes, routed, routing

row   rows, rowed, rowing, rower, rowers

rubber   rubbers, rubbery, rubberize, rubberizing

rudder   rudders

rude   ruder, rudest, rudely, rudeness

ruin   ruins, ruined, ruining, ruinous, ruinously

rule   rules, ruled, ruling, rulings, ruler, rulers

run   runs, ran, running, runner, runners

runaway   runaways

rural   rurally

rush   rushes, rushed, rushing

rustle   rustles, rustled, rustling, rustler, rustlers

ruth   ruthless, ruthlessly, ruthlessness

S

sack sacks, sacked, sacking

sacrifice sacrifices, sacrificed, sacrificing, sacrificial

sad sadder, saddest, sadden, sadly, sadness

saddle saddles, saddled, saddling

safe safes, safer, safest, safely, safeness, safety

sail sails, sailed, sailing, sailor, sailors

salad salads

salary salaries, salaried

salesperson salespeople

salt salts, salted, salting, salty, saltier, saltiest

salute salutes, saluted, saluting, salutation, salutations

same sameness

sample samples, sampled, sampling, sampler, samplers

sand sandy, sandier, sandiest

sandwich sandwiches, sandwiched, sandwiching

sanitary sanitarily, sanitation, sanitize, sanitizes, sanitized, sanitizing

sarcasm sarcastic, sarcastically

satellite satellites

satisfy satisfies, satisfied, satisfying, satisfyingly, satisfactory, satisfactorily, satisfaction

saturate saturates, saturated, saturating, saturation

Saturday Sat.

sauce sauces, sauced, saucing, saucer, saucers, saucy

savage savages, savagely, savageness

save saves, saved, saving, savings, saver, savers

say says, said, saying

scale scales, scaled, scaling, scaly

scant scanty, scantly, scantness, scantily

scar scars, scarred, scarring

scarce scarcer, scarcest, scarcely, scarceness, scarcity, scarcities

scare scares, scared, scaring, scary, scarier, scariest, scariness

scarf scarves

scatter scatters, scattered, scattering

scene scenes, scenic, scenery, scenario, scenarios

scent scents, scented, scenting

schedule schedules, scheduled, scheduling, scheduler, schedulers

scheme schemes, schemed, scheming, schemer, schemers, schematic, schematics

scholar   scholars, scholarly, scholarship, scholarships, scholastic, scholastics, scholastically

school   schools

schoolmate   schoolmates

science   sciences, scientist, scientists, scientific, scientifically

scissors

scold   scolds, scolded, scolding

score   scores, scored, scoring, scorer, scorers

scorn   scorns, scorned, scorning, scornful, scornfully, scornfulness

scowl   scowls, scowled, scowling

scramble   scrambles, scrambled, scrambling, scrambler, scramblers

scrap   scraps, scrapped, scrapping, scrapper, scrappers, scrappy, scrappier, scrappiest

scrape   scrapes, scraped, scraping, scraper, scrapers

scratch   scratches, scratched, scratching, scratchy, scratchier, scratchiest, scratchiness, scratcher, scratchers

scream   screams, screamed, screaming, screamer, screamers

screwdriver   screwdrivers

scrub   scrubs, scrubbed, scrubbing, scrubber, scrubbers

sea   seas

seal   seals, sealed, sealing, sealer, sealers

search   searches, searched, searching, searchingly

seashore   seashores

season   seasons, seasoned, seasoning, seasonable, seasonal, seasonably, seasonally

seat   seats, seated, seating

seclude   secludes, secluded, secluding, seclusive, seclusion

second   seconds, seconded, seconding, secondly

secret   secrets, secretive, secretly, secrecy

secretary   secretaries, secretarial

section   sections, sectioned, sectioning, sectional, sectionally, sectionalize

secure   secures, secured, securing, securely, security, securities

see   sees, saw, seen, seeing

seed   seeds, seeded, seeding, seeder, seeders, seedling, seedlings

seem   seems, seemed, seeming, seemingly

segment   segments, segmented, segmenting, segmentary, segmental, segmentation, segmentations

segregate   segregates, segregated, segregating, segregative, segregation, segregationist, segregationists

seize   seizes, seized, seizing, seizure, seizures

seldom   seldomly

select   selects, selected, selecting, selective, selectively, selectness, selection, selections

self-centered   self-centeredly, self-centeredness

self-conscious   self-consciously, self-consciousness

selfish   selfishly, selfishness

selfless   selflessly, selflessness

sell   sells, sold, selling, seller, sellers

semester   semesters

senate   senates, senator, senators

send   sends, sent, sending, sender, senders

senior   seniors, seniority

sensation   sensations, sensational, sensationalize, sensationally

sense   senses, sensed, sensing, sensible, sensibly, sensibility, senseless, sensory

sensitive   sensitively, sensitivity, sensitivities

sentence   sentences, sentenced, sentencing

sentiment   sentiments, sentimental, sentimentally, sentimentalist, sentimentalists

separate   separates, separated, separating, separately, separation, separations, separateness, separable, separator, separators

September   Sept.

sequence sequences, sequenced, sequencing, sequent, sequential, sequentially

serious seriously, seriousness

serve serves, served, serving, server, servers, servant, servants, service, services

session sessions

set sets, setting, settings

settle settles, settled, settling, settler, settlers, settlement, settlements

seven sevens, seventh, sevenths

several

severe severer, severest, severely, severity, severeness

sew sews, sewed, sewn, sewing

shack shacks

shade shades, shaded, shading, shadiness, shady, shadier, shadiest

shadow shadows, shadowed, shadowing, shadowy

shaft shafts

shake shakes, shook, shaking, shaken, shaky, shakier, shakiest, shakily, shaker, shakers

shall

shame shames, shamed, shaming, shameful, shamefully, shameless, shamelessly, shamelessness

shape shapes, shaped, shaping, shapely, shapeless

share

share   shares, shared, sharing

shark   sharks

sharp   sharper, sharpest, sharply, sharpness, sharpen, sharpens, sharpened, sharpening

she   she's

shed   sheds, shedding, shedder, shedders

sheep   sheepish, sheepishly

sheer   sheerly, sheerness

sheet   sheets, sheeting

shell   shells, shelled, shelling

shelter   shelters, sheltered, sheltering

sheriff   sheriffs

shield   shields, shielded, shielding

shine   shines, shined, shone, shining, shiny, shinier, shiniest

ship   ships, shipped, shipping, shipment, shipments, shipper, shippers

shirt   shirts

shock   shocks, shocked, shocking, shockingly, shocker, shockers

shoe   shoes

shop   shops, shopped, shopping, shopper, shoppers

shore   shores

short   shorter, shortest, shortly, shorten, shortens, shortened, shortening, shortness

should   shouldn't

shoulder   shoulders, shouldered,
   shouldering

shout   shouts, shouted, shouting

shovel   shovels, shoveled, shoveling

show   shows, showed, shown, showing,
   showy

shower   showers, showered, showering

shut   shuts, shutting, shutter, shutters

sick   sicker, sickest, sickly, sicken,
   sickens, sickened, sickening, sickeningly,
   sickness, sicknesses

side   sides, sided, siding

sidewalk   sidewalks

sideways

sigh   sighs, sighed, sighing

sight   sights, sighted, sighting, sightless

sign   signs, signed, signing, signer, signers

signal   signals, signaled, signaling,
   signaler, signalers

signature   signatures

signify   signifies, signified, signifying,
   signifiable, significant, significantly,
   significance, significancy

silent   silently, silence, silences, silenced,
   silencing, silencer, silencers

silk   silks, silkier, silkiest, silky, silken

silly   sillier, silliest, silliness

silver　silvers, silvered, silvery

similar　similarly, similarity, simile, similes

simple　simply, simpler, simplest, simplicity, simplify, simplifies, simplified, simplifying, simplifier, simplifiers

since

sincere　sincerely, sincerest, sincerity

sing　sings, sang, sung, singing, singer, singers

single　singles, singled, singling, singly, singular, singulars, singularity, singularly

sink　sinks, sank, sunk, sunken, sinking

sir　sirs

sister　sisters

sit　sits, sat, sitting, sitter, sitters

situate　situates, situated, situating, situation, situations

six　sixes, sixth, sixths

sixteen　sixteens, sixteenth

size　sizes, sized, sizing

skate　skates, skated, skating, skater, skaters

skeleton　skeletons, skeletal, skeletals

sketch　sketches, sketched, sketching, sketchy, sketcher, sketchers, sketchier, sketchiest, sketchily, sketchiness

ski   skis, skied, skiing, skier, skiers

skid   skids, skidded, skidding

skill   skills, skilled, skillful, skillfully, skillfulness

skim   skims, skimmed, skimming, skimmer, skimmers

skin   skins, skinned, skinning

skirt   skirts, skirted, skirting

skit   skits, skittish, skittishly

sky   skies

sled   sleds, sledding

sleep   sleeps, slept, sleeping, sleeper, sleepers, sleepy, sleepier, sleepiest, sleepily

sleeve   sleeves, sleeved, sleeveless

sleigh   sleighs, sleighed, sleighing

slice   slices, sliced, slicing, slicer, slicers

slide   slides, slid, sliding, slider, sliders

slight   slights, slighted, slighting, slighter, slightest, slightly, slightness

slip   slips, slipped, slipping, slippery, slipperier, slipperiest, slipperiness, slipper, slippers

slither   slithers, slithered, slithering, slithery

slow   slows, slowed, slowing, slower, slowest, slowly, slowness

slumber   slumbers, slumbered, slumbering, slumberer, slumberers

small   smaller, smallest, smallness

smash   smashes, smashed, smashing,
smashingly

smear   smears, smeared, smearing

smell   smells, smelled, smelling, smelly,
smellier, smelliest

smile   smiles, smiled, smiling

smirk   smirks, smirked, smirking,
smirker

smoke   smokes, smoked, smoking, smoky,
smokier, smokiest, smoker, smokers

smolder   smolders, smoldered, smoldering

smooth   smooths, smoothed, smoothing,
smoother, smoothest, smoothly,
smoothness

smother   smothers, smothered, smothering

snag   snags, snagged, snagging

snake   snakes

snap   snaps, snapped, snapping, snapper,
snappers

sneak   sneaks, sneaked, sneaking, sneaky,
sneakier, sneakiest

sneaker   sneakers

sneeze   sneezes, sneezed, sneezing

snoop   snoops, snooped, snooping, snooper,
snoopers, snoopy, snoopier, snoopiest

snow   snows, snowed, snowing, snowy,
snowier, snowiest

snowball snowballs, snowballed, snowballing

so

so-called

soak soaks, soaked, soaking

soap soaps, soaped, soaping, soapy, soapier, soapiest

sob sobs, sobbed, sobbing

social socials, socially, sociable, sociably, sociableness, society, societies, societal, socialize, socializes, socialized, socializing, socialism, socialist, socialists, socialization, sociability

sock socks, socked, socking

soft soften, softer, softest, softly, softness

soil soils, soiled, soiling

sole soles, soled, soling

solemn solemnly, solemnize, solemnify, solemnity, solemnness

solid solids, solidity, solidify, solidifies, solidified, solidifying, solidifier, solidifiers, solidarity, solidarities

solitary solitarily, solitude

solo solos, soloing, soloed, soloist, soloists

solution solutions

solve solves, solved, solving, solvable, solver, solvers

some somebody, somehow, someone, something, sometimes, somewhat, somewhere

somersault somersaults, somersaulted, somersaulting

son sons

song songs, songster, songsters

soon sooner, soonest

sore sores, sorer, sorest, sorely, soreness

sorrow sorrows, sorrowed, sorrowing, sorrowful, sorrowfully, sorrowfulness

sorry sorrier, sorriest, sorrily

sort sorts, sorted, sorting, sorter, sorters

sound sounds, sounded, sounding, sounder, soundest

sour sours, soured, sourest, souring, sourly, sourness

source sources

south southward, southerly, southern, southerner, southerners

space spaces, spaced, spacing, spacer, spacers, spacious, spaciously, spaciousness

spade spades, spaded, spading

spare spares, spared, sparing, sparingly, spareness

sparkle sparkles, sparkled, sparkling, sparkler, sparklers

sparrow sparrows

speak speaks, spoke, spoken, speaking, speaker, speakers

special specials, specialize, specializes, specialized, specializing, specialization, specialty, specialties, specialist, specialists

species

specify specifies, specified, specifying, specific, specifics, specifically, specification, specifications, specificity, specificities, specifier, specifiers

specimen specimens

speech speeches, speechless, speechlessness

speed speeds, speeded, sped, speeding, speedy, speedier, speediest, speedily, speeder, speeders

spell spells, spelled, spelling, speller, spellers

spend spends, spent, spending, spendable, spender, spenders

sphere spheres, sphered, spherical

spill spills, spilled, spilling, spillage

spin spins, spun, spinning, spinner, spinners

spirit spirits, spirited, spiritual, spirituality, spiritless

spite spites, spited, spiting, spiteful, spitefully, spitefulness

splash splashes, splashed, splashing, splashy, splashier, splashiest, splasher, splashers

splendid splendidly, splendidness, splendor, splendors, splendorous, splendorously

split splits, splitting, splitter, splitters

spoil spoils, spoiled, spoiling, spoiler, spoilers

spoon spoons, spooned, spooning, spooner, spooners

sport sports, sported, sporting

spot spots, spotted, spotting, spotter, spotters

sprawl sprawls, sprawled, sprawling

spray sprays, sprayed, spraying, sprayer, sprayers

spread spreads, spreading, spreader, spreaders

spring springs, sprang, sprung, springing, springy, springier, springiest, springiness

sprinkle sprinkles, sprinkled, sprinkling, sprinkler, sprinklers

spry spryly, sprier, spriest, spryness

squall squalls, squalled, squalling

square squares, squared, squaring, squarest, squarish, squarely, squareness

squash squashes, squashed, squashing, squashy, squashier, squashiest, squashiness

squeeze squeezes, squeezed, squeezing, squeezable, squeezer, squeezers

squirrel   squirrels, squirreled, squirreling

stable   stables, stabled, stabling, stabler, stablest, stability

stack   stacks, stacked, stacking

staff   staffs, staffed, staffing

stair   stairs

stairway   stairways, stairwell, stairwells

stake   stakes, staked, staking

stalk   stalks, stalked, stalking, stalker, stalkers

stamp   stamps, stamped, stamping, stamper, stampers

stand   stands, stood, standing

standard   standards, standardize, standardized

star   stars

stare   stares, stared, staring, staringly, starer, starers

start   starts, started, starting, starter, starters

startle   startles, startled, startling

starve   starves, starved, starving, starvation

state   states, stated, stating, stately, statelier, stateliest

station   stations, stationed, stationing, stationary

stationery

statue statues, statuette, statuettes, statuary

stay stays, stayed, staying

steady steadies, steadied, steadying, steadier, steadiest, steadily, steadiness

steal steals, stole, stolen, stealing, stealer, stealers

steam steams, steamed, steaming, steamer, steamers, steamy, steamier, steamiest

steel steels, steely, steelier, steeliest

steep steeper, steepest, steeply

steer steers, steered, steering, steerable, steerer, steerers, steerage

step steps, stepped, stepping

sterile sterility, sterilize, sterilizes, sterilized, sterilizing, sterilization

stick sticks, stuck, sticking, sticky, stickier, stickiest, stickiness

still stillness

stimulate stimulates, stimulated, stimulating, stimulative, stimulation, stimulus, stimulant, stimulants, stimulator, stimulators

sting stings, stung, stinging, stinger, stingers

stingy stingier, stingiest, stingily, stinginess

stir stirs, stirred, stirring, stirrer, stirrers

stitch   stitches, stitched, stitching, stitcher, stitchers

stocking   stockings

stomach   stomachs, stomached, stomaching

stone   stones, stoned, stoning

stoop   stoops, stooped, stooping

stop   stops, stopped, stopping, stopper, stoppers

store   stores, stored, storing

storm   storms, stormed, storming, stormy, stormier, stormiest

story   stories, storied

stove   stoves

straight   straighter, straightest, straightly, straightness, straighten, straightens, straightened, straightening, straightener, straighteners

strain   strains, strained, straining, strainer, strainers

strange   strangely, stranger, strangest, strangeness, strangers

strategy   strategies, strategic, strategically, strategist, strategists, stratagem

straw   straws

stray   strays, strayed, straying

stream   streams, streamed, streaming, streamer, streamers

street   streets

strength   strengths, strengthen, strengthens, strengthened, strengthening, strengthener, strengtheners

strenuous   strenuously, strenuousness

stretch   stretches, stretched, stretching, stretchable, stretchy, stretchier, stretchiest, stretchiness, stretcher, stretchers

strict   stricter, strictest, strictly, strictness

strike   strikes, struck, striking, strikingly, striker, strikers

string   strings, strung, stringing, stringy, stringier, stringiest

strip   strips, stripped, stripping, stripper, strippers

stroll   strolls, strolled, strolling, stroller, strollers

strong   stronger, strongest, strongly

struggle   struggles, struggled, struggling, struggler, strugglers

stubborn   stubborner, stubbornest, stubbornly, stubbornness

student   students

study   studies, studied, studying, studious, studiously, studiousness

stuff   stuffs, stuffed, stuffing, stuffy, stuffier, stuffiest

stump   stumps, stumped, stumping, stumpy, stumpier, stumpiest

stupid stupider, stupidest, stupidity, stupidly

style styles, styled, styling, stylish, stylishly, stylishness, stylist, stylists

subject subjects, subjected, subjecting, subjective, subjectively

submarine submarines

submerge submerges, submerged, submerging, submergence

submit submits, submitted, submitting, submittance

subscribe subscribes, subscribed, subscribing, subscriber, subscribers, subscription, subscriptions

substance substances, substantial, substantially, substantiate, substantiates, substantiated, substantiating, substantive, substantiation

substitute substitutes, substituted, substituting, substitutable, substitution, substitutions, substitutional

suburb suburbs, suburban, suburbanite, suburbanites, suburbia

succeed succeeds, succeeded, succeeding

success successful, successfully, successfulness, succession, successive, successor, successors

such

sudden suddenly, suddenness

suffer suffers, suffered, suffering, sufferer, sufferers, sufferance

suffice suffices, sufficed, sufficing, sufficient, sufficiency, sufficiently

suggest suggests, suggested, suggesting, suggestible, suggestive, suggestively, suggestion, suggestions

suit suits, suited, suiting, suitable, suitably, suitability

suite suites

sulk sulks, sulked, sulking, sulker, sulkers, sulky, sulkier, sulkiest, sulkily, sulkiness

sullen sullenly, sullenness

sultry sultrier, sultriest, sultriness

sum sums, summed, summing

summary summaries, summarized, summarizes, summarizing

summer summers, summery

summons summonses, summoned, summoning, summoner, summoners

sun suns, sunned, sunning, sunny, sunnier, sunniest, sunniness

Sunday Sun.

superb superbly, superbness

superior superiors, superiority

supervise supervises, supervised, supervising, supervision, supervisor, supervisors, supervisory

supper suppers

supplement supplements, supplemented, supplementing, supplemental, supplementary, supplementation

supply supplies, supplied, supplying, supplier, suppliers

support supports, supported, supporting, supportable, supportive, supportively, supporter, supporters

suppose supposes, supposed, supposing, supposedly, supposition, suppositions

supreme supremely, supremacy, supremeness

sure surely, surer, surest, sureness

surface surfaces, surfaced, surfacing

surgeon surgeons

surplus

surprise surprises, surprised, surprising, surprisingly

surrender surrenders, surrendered, surrendering

surround surrounds, surrounded, surrounding, surroundings

survey surveys, surveyed, surveying, surveyor, surveyors

suspect suspects, suspected, suspecting, suspicion, suspicions, suspicious, suspiciously, suspiciousness

suspend suspends, suspended, suspending, suspense, suspension, suspensions, suspenders

swallow swallows, swallowed, swallowing

sway   sways, swayed, swaying, swayer, swayers

sweater   sweaters

sweep   sweeps, swept, sweeping, sweeper, sweepers

sweet   sweets, sweeter, sweetest, sweetly, sweeten, sweetness

swell   swells, swelled, swelling, swollen, swollenly

swift   swifter, swiftest, swiftly, swiftness

swim   swims, swam, swum, swimming, swimmer, swimmers, swimmingly

swing   swings, swung, swinging, swinger, swingers

switch   switches, switched, switching, switcher, switchers

swivel   swivels, swiveled, swiveling

sword   swords

syllable   syllables, syllabic, syllabicate, syllabication

symbol   symbols, symbolic, symbolically, symbolism, symbolize, symbolizes, symbolized, symbolizing

sympathy   sympathies, sympathize, sympathizes, sympathized, sympathizing, sympathizer, sympathetic, sympathetically

system   systems, systematic, systematize, systematized, systematizing, systemic

T

table   tables, tabled, tabling

tablet   tablets

tackle   tackles, tackled, tackling, tackler, tacklers

tail   tails, tailed, tailing

tailor   tailors, tailored, tailoring

take   takes, took, taken, taking, taker, takers

talent   talents, talented

talk   talks, talked, talking, talkative, talker, talkers

tall   taller, tallest

tan   tans, tanned, tanning, tanner, tanners, tannest

tar   tars, tarred, tarring

tariff   tariffs

tarnish   tarnishes, tarnished, tarnishing

taxi   taxis, taxied, taxiing

teach   teaches, taught, teaching, teachable, teacher, teachers

team   teams, teamed, teaming, teamster, teamsters

tear   tears, tore, torn, teared, tearing, tearful, tearfully

telecommunication   telecommunications

telegraph telegraphs, telegraphed, telegraphing, telegraphic, telegrapher, telegraphy

telephone telephones, telephoned, telephoning

television televisions, televise, televises, televised, televising

tell tells, told, telling, teller, tellers

temper tempers, tempered, tempering, temperament, temperaments, temperamental, temperamentally

temperature temperatures, temperate, temperately

tempo tempos, tempi

temporary temporarily, temporariness

tempt tempts, tempted, tempting, temptable, temptation, temptations, tempter, tempters

ten tens, tenth

tend tends, tended, tending, tendency, tendencies, tender

tennis

tent tents

term terms, termed, terming

terrible terribly, terribleness

territory territories, territorial, territorialize, territorializes, territorialized

terror terrors, terrorize, terrorizes, terrorized, terrorizing, terrorizer, terrorism, terrorist, terrorists

test tests, tested, testing, tester, testers

textile textiles

texture textures, textured, textural, texturally

than

thank thanks, thanked, thanking, thankful, thankfully, thankless, thanksgiving

the

theater theaters, theatrical, theatrically, theatrics

theft thefts

their theirs

them themselves

then

theory theories, theorize, theorizes, theorized, theorizing, theorist, theorists

therapy therapies, therapeutic, therapist, therapists

there

thermometer thermometers

they they're

thick thicker, thickest, thickly, thickness

thief thieves, thieved, thieving, thievery, thievish, thievishly

thin thinner, thinness, thinnest, thinly, thins, thinned, thinning

thing   things

think   thinks, thinking, thinker, thinkers

thirst   thirsts, thirsted, thirsting, thirsty, thirstier, thirstiest, thirstily, thirstiness

thirteen   thirteens, thirteenth

thirty   thirties, thirtieth

this   that, these, those

thorough   thoroughly, thoroughness

though

thought   thoughts, thoughtful, thoughtfully, thoughtfulness, thoughtless, thoughtlessly, thoughtlessness

thousand   thousands, thousandth

thread   threads, threaded, threading, threader, threaders

threat   threats, threaten, threatens, threatened, threatening, threateningly

three   threes, third, thirds

thrill   thrills, thrilled, thrilling, thrillingly, thriller, thrillers

throat   throats, throaty, throatier, throatiest, throatily

throne   thrones

through

throw   throws, threw, thrown, throwing, thrower, throwers

thrust   thrusts, thrust, thrusting, thruster, thrusters

thumb   thumbs, thumbed, thumbing

thunder   thunders, thundered, thundering, thundery, thunderous, thunderously

Thursday   Thurs.

ticket   tickets, ticketed, ticketing, ticketer, ticketers

tickle   tickles, tickled, tickling, ticklish, ticklishly, ticklishness, tickler, ticklers

tide   tides, tidal

tie   ties, tied, tying

tight   tights, tighten, tightens, tightened, tightening, tighter, tightest, tightly, tightness

tile   tiles, tiled, tiling, tiler, tilers

time   times, timed, timing, timer, timers

timetable   timetables

timid   timidly, timidity, timidness

tin   tins, tinned, tinning, tinny

tiny   tinier, tiniest

tire   tires, tired, tiring, tireless, tirelessly, tiresome, tiresomely, tiredness

to   too

today

toe   toes

together   togetherness

tolerate   tolerates, tolerated, tolerating, tolerant, tolerable, tolerably, tolerantly, tolerance, tolerances, toleration

tomato   tomatoes

ton   tons

tone   tones, toned, toning, toneless, toner, toners

tongue   tongues

tonight

tool   tools, tooled, tooling

tooth   teeth, toothy, toothier, toothiest, toothless

top   tops, topped, topping

topic   topics, topical, topically

torment   torments, tormented, tormenting, tormentor, tormentors

torrent   torrents, torrential, torrentially

torrid   torridly, torridness

toss   tosses, tossed, tossing

total   totals, totaled, totaling, totally, totality, totalize, totalizes, totalized, totalizing, totalization

touch   touches, touched, touching, touchy, touchier, touchiest, touchable

tough   tougher, toughest, toughly, toughen, toughens, toughened, toughening, toughness

tour   tours, toured, touring, tourist, tourists, tourism

tournament   tournaments, tourney, tourneys

toward   towards

towel   towels, toweled, toweling

tower   towers, towered, towering

town   towns

toy   toys, toyed, toying

trace   traces, traced, tracing, tracer, tracers

track   tracks, tracked, tracking, tracker, trackers

trade   trades, traded, trading, trader, traders

tradition   traditions, traditional, traditionally, traditionalism, traditionalist, traditionalists

traffic   trafficked, trafficking

tragedy   tragedies, tragic, tragical, tragically

trail   trails, trailed, trailing, trailer, trailers

train   trains, trained, training, trainers, trainers

transfer   transfers, transferred, transferring, transferable, transferability, transferal, transferals, transference

transmit   transmits, transmitted, transmitting, transmittable, transmitter, transmitters, transmission, transmissions

transport   transports, transported, transporting, transportable, transportability, transportation, transporter, transporters

169

trap

trap traps, trapped, trapping, trapper, trappers

trash trashy, trashier, trashiest

travel travels, traveled, traveling, traveler, travelers

treasure treasures, treasured, treasuring, treasury, treasuries, treasurer, treasurers

treat treats, treated, treating, treatable, treatment, treatments

treaty treaties

tree trees

tremendous tremendously

trial trials

tribe tribes, tribal

tribute tributes, tributary, tributaries

trick tricks, tricked, tricking, tricky, trickier, trickiest, trickster, tricksters

trifle trifles, trifled, trifling

trim trims, trimmed, trimming, trimmer, trimmest, trimly, trimness

trip trips, tripped, tripping

triumph triumphs, triumphed, triumphing, triumphant, triumphantly

troop troops, trooped, trooping, trooper, troopers

trophy trophies

trouble troubles, troubled, troubling, troublesome

trout   trout

truck   trucks, trucked, trucking, trucker, truckers

true   truer, truest, truly, trueness

trunk   trunks

trust   trusts, trusted, trusting, trustful, trustfully, trustless, trustiness

truth   truths, truthful, truthfully, truthfulness

try   tries, tried, trying

Tuesday Tues.

turn   turns, turned, turning

turtle   turtles

twelve   twelves, twelfth

twenty   twenties, twentieth

twenty-five   twenty-fives, twenty-fifth

twig   twigs

twilight   twilights

twin   twins

twist   twists, twisted, twisting, twister, twisters

two   twos, twice

typewriter   typewriters, typewrite, typewrites, typewritten, typewriting

typical   typically

typify   typifies, typified, typifying

U

ugly uglier, ugliest, ugliness

umbrella umbrellas

umpire umpires, umpired, umpiring

unanimous unanimously, unanimity

unavoidable unavoidably

unaware unawares

uncertain uncertainly, uncertainty, uncertainties, uncertainness

unclaimed

uncle uncles

uncomfortable uncomfortably

uncommon uncommonly, uncommonness

unconscious unconsciously, unconsciousness

under

underdog underdogs

undergraduate undergraduates

undergrowth

underrate underrates, underrated, underrating

undertake undertakes, undertook, undertaken, undertaking, undertaker, undertakers

undisputed undisputedly

undoubted undoubtedly

uneasy uneasier, uneasiest, uneasily, uneasiness

uneventful uneventfully

unexpected unexpectedly, unexpectedness

unfortunate unfortunately

uniform uniforms, uniformed, uniformly

unify unifies, unified, unifying

unimaginable unimaginableness

union unions, unionize, unionizes, unionized, unionizing, unionizer, unionizers

unit units

unite unites, united, uniting, unity, unities

universe universes, universal, universally, universalize, universalized, universalizing

university universities

unjust unjustly, unjustness

unless

unlimited

unload unloads, unloaded, unloading

unlock unlocks, unlocked, unlocking

unnecessary unnecessarily

unoccupied

unpack unpacks, unpacked, unpacking

unpleasant unpleasantly, unpleasantness

unpredictable unpredictably

unruly   unrulier, unruliest, unruliness

until

unusual   unusually, unusualness

unwilling   unwillingly, unwillingness

unwise   unwisely

unworthy   unworthier, unworthiest, unworthily, unworthiness

unyielding

up   upper, upward, upwards

uphold   upholds, upheld, upholding, upholder, upholders

upon

upright   uprightly, uprightness

uprising   uprisings

upstairs

urban   urbanism, urbanite, urbanites

urge   urges, urged, urging, urgent, urgently, urgency

us

use   uses, used, using, useful, usefully, usefulness, usable, usage, usages, useless, uselessly, uselessness

usher   ushers, ushered, ushering

usual   usually, usualness

utilize   utilizes, utilized, utilizing, utilization, utility, utilities

utter   utters, uttered, uttering, utterance, utterable, utterly, utmost, uttermost

V

vacant   vacantly, vacantness, vacancy, vacancies, vacate, vacates, vacated, vacating

vacation   vacations, vacationer, vacationers

vacuum   vacuums, vacuumed, vacuuming

vague   vaguer, vaguest, vaguely, vagueness

vain   vainly, vainness, vanity, vanities

valentine   valentines

valley   valleys

value   values, valued, valuing, valuably, valueless, valuate, valuable, valuables, valuation

vanish   vanishes, vanished, vanishing

vary   varies, varied, varying, various, variously, variable, variety, varieties, variant, variation

vast   vaster, vastest, vastly, vastness

vegetable   vegetables

vegetate   vegetates, vegetated, vegetating, vegetation, vegetarian, vegetarians

velvet   velvets, velvety, velvetiness, velveteen

vengeance   vengeful, vengefully

venture   ventures, ventured, venturing, venturer, venturers, venturesome, venturesomely

verify verifies, verified, verifying, verification, verifiable, verifier, verifiers

versus vs.

vertical vertically, verticalness

very

vessel vessels

vice vices

vicinity vicinities

vicious viciously, viciousness

victim victims, victimize, victimizes, victimized, victimizing

victory victories, victorious, victoriously, victoriousness, victor, victors

view views, viewed, viewing, viewer, viewers

viewpoint viewpoints

vigor vigorous, vigorously, vigorousness

village villages, villager, villagers

violent violently, violence

virtue virtues, virtuous, virtuously

visible visibly, visibility, visibilities, visibleness

visit visits, visited, visiting, visitation, visitor, visitors

visual visually

vital vitally, vitalize, vitalizes, vitalized, vitalizing, vitality

vocation vocations, vocational, vocationally

voice voices, voiced, voicing, voiceless, voicelessness

volcano volcanoes, volcanic, volcanically

volume volumes, voluminous, voluminously

volunteer volunteers, volunteered, volunteering, voluntary, voluntarily

vote votes, voted, voting, voter, voters

vouch vouches, vouched, vouching, voucher, vouchers

vow vows, vowed, vowing

voyage voyages, voyaged, voyaging, voyager, voyagers

vulgar vulgarly, vulgarity, vulgarities

W

wade wades, waded, wading

wager wagers, wagered, wagering, wagerer, wagerers

waist waists

wait waits, waited, waiting, waiter, waiters, waitress, waitresses

wake wakes, waked, woke, waking, waken, wakens, wakened, wakening

walk walks, walked, walking, walker, walkers

wall walls, walled

wander wanders, wandered, wandering, wanderer, wanderers

want wants, wanted, wanting, wantingly

warehouse warehouses, warehoused, warehousing

warm warms, warmed, warming, warmer, warmest, warmly, warmth

warrant warrants, warranted, warranting, warrantable, warranty, warranties

was

wash washes, washed, washing, washer, washers

waste wastes, wasted, wasting, wasteful, wastefully

watch watches, watched, watching, watcher, watchers

water waters, watered, watering, watery

way ways

we we're, we've

weak weaker, weakest, weakly, weakness

wealth wealthy, wealthier, wealthiest, wealthily, wealthiness

wear wears, wore, worn, wearing

weary wearies, wearied, wearying, wearier, weariest, wearily, weariness

weather

weave weaves, weaved, weaving, wove, woven, weaver, weavers

Wednesday Wed.

weed weeds, weeded, weeding, weedy, weedier, weediest

week weeks, weekly, weekday, weekdays, weekend, weekends

weigh weighs, weighed, weighing, weigher, weight, weights, weighty, weightier, weightiest, weightless, weightlessness

weird weirdest, weirdly, weirdness

welcome welcomes, welcomed, welcoming

welfare

well wells

went

were weren't

west western, westerner, westerners, westerly, westward

wet wetter, wettest, wetness

whale

whale   whales, whaling, whaler, whalers

what

wheat

wheel   wheels, wheeled, wheeling

when

where

whether

which

while

whimper   whimpers, whimpered,
  whimpering

whip   whips, whipped, whipping

whirl   whirls, whirled, whirling,
  whirlingly

whisper   whispers, whispered, whispering,
  whisperer, whisperers

whistle   whistles, whistled, whistling,
  whistler, whistlers

white   whiter, whitest, whited, whiting

who   whom, whose, whoever, whomever

whole   wholes, wholesome, wholly

why

wicked   wickedly, wickedness

wide   wider, widest, wideness, widely, widen

width   widths

wild   wilder, wildest, wildly, wilds,
  wildness, wilderness

180

will would, wouldn't

win wins, won, winning, winner, winners

wind winds, wound, winding, windy, windier, windiest

window windows

wing wings, winged, winging, wingless

winter winters, wintered, wintering

wire wires, wired, wiring

wise wiser, wisest, wisely, wisdom

wish wishes, wished, wishing, wisher, wishers

with without

withdraw withdraws, withdrew, withdrawn, withdrawing, withdrawal, withdrawals

wither withers, withered, withering, witheringly

witness witnesses, witnessed, witnessing

woman women, womanly

won't will not

wonder wonders, wondered, wondering, wonderful, wonderfully, wondrous, wondrously

wood woods, wooded, wooden, woody

wool wools, woolen, woolens, wooly, woolier, wooliest

word words, worded, wording, wordy, wordier, wordiest

work   works, worked, working, worker, worskers

world   worlds, worldly

worry   worries, worried, worrying, worrier, worriers

worse   worst

worth   worthy, worthier, worthiest, worthiness, worthless, worthlessness

wrap   wraps, wrapped, wrapping, wrapper, wrappers

wreck   wrecks, wrecked, wrecking, wreckage, wrecker, wreckers

wrench   wrenches, wrenched, wrenching

wrestle   wrestles, wrestled, wrestling, wrestler, wrestlers

wrist   wrists

write   writes, wrote, written, writing, writer, writers

wrong   wrongs, wronged, wronging, wrongly

Y

yard   yards, yardage, yardages

year   years, yearly

yell   yells, yelled, yelling, yeller, yellers

yellow   yellows, yellowed, yellowing

yes

yesterday   yesterdays

yet

yield   yields, yielded, yielding, yieldingly

you   your

young   younger, youngest, youngster, youngsters

yourself   yourselves

youth   youths, youthful, youthfully, youthfulness

Z

zoo zoos

To Order Additional Copies of Wordfinder Please Complete:

Mall Form to: D.C. Heath and Company
2700 North Richardt Avenue
P. O. Box 19309
Indianapolis, IN 46219

Code #	Title	Quantity	Unit Price*	Total Price
20711-X	WORDFINDER		3.95	

BILL TO:

Purchase Order # _____

School/Organization _____

Address _____

City _____ State ___ Zip ___

Attention (must be given) _____

Telephone ( ) _____

SHIP TO:

School/Organization _____

Address _____

City _____ State ___ Zip ___

Attention (must be given) _____

*Price is subject to change without notice